Television at the

Crossroads

Television at the Crossroads

Stefano Marzano, editor

First published in Great Britain in 1995 by

ACADEMY EDITIONS

An imprint of

ACADEMY GROUP LTD

42 Leinster Gardens London W2 3 AN

Member of the VCH Publishing Group

ISBN 1 85490 425 6

Distributed to the trade in the United States of

America by ST MARTIN'S PRESS

175 Fifth Avenue, New York, NY 10010

Television at the Crossroads

Alessandro Mendini

Andrea Branzi

Stefano Marzano

Contents

Television at the Crossroads

Television at the Crossroads:

The Quest for New Qualities

Stefano Marzano

Gift from the Gods or Trojan Horse?

One of the most potent symbols and vehicles of our current high-tech society is the television set. The automobile, the aeroplane and radio have clearly left no one's life entirely untouched, but it is arguably television that has affected people's *minds* most deeply. Around the globe, the television set provides a very literal window on the world outside, liberating at the same time the inner, private world of the imagination.

But is television truly a gift from the gods? Or is it a Trojan Horse, coming into our homes as a deceiver, providing what at first seems to be harmless entertainment and information, but which ultimately turns out to have undermined the fabric of our societies, the integrity of our brains and the health of our bodies?

Television has been regarded in both these ways since it began to penetrate our lives on a large scale almost fifty years ago. Now, a generation has grown up which has hardly known life without it. But just how radically television has changed our modes of living, how it itself has changed over the years, and how it may yet affect our deeper experience of life is only just beginning to become clear.

Television, *quo vadis?* And viewer, *quem videbis?* Where is the medium going, and what shall we, as viewers, be seeing in the future? These are the questions addressed by the contributors to this book. Each author focuses on different aspects of television, approaching the topic from the standpoint of his own area of expertise. The aim is not to find definitive answers, but to present what may perhaps best be described as a collection of musings, meditations or brain-stormings. They were originally inspired by a series of design workshops held in Italy and Holland. We hope that, in turn, they may inspire a wider public to take an active part in shaping the future of television as it enters a new phase of its existence. But we believe almost anyone who watches television should find food for thought in this volume.

Before we rush on

The technology of television is now over sixty years old, and with the convergence of television, computer and telecommunications technology about to result in an explosion of new applications, the time is ripe for us to review the state of the art and take a considered look towards the future. In terms of social and psychological developments, we can now trace the effects of television on a whole generation, seeing how the medium has increasingly come to dominate our lives – for better and for worse. In terms of design, we have also seen the set itself develop in unexpected directions. From a cumbersome box with a tiny screen and dials it has been transformed into a whole range of models of varying sizes in which the screen has become almost all we see and the controls have moved from the set itself to settle in the hand of the viewer.

Home, Head and Highway

Considering television from the sociological viewpoint, Francesco Morace, ('The Magical Mirror of Everyday Life') points to the dual nature of television. On the one hand, it exerts a tremendous influence on the social, spatial and temporal organisation of our lives, both in relation to others and to the television set itself. On the other hand, it reflects those changes as they happen. Its increasing mobility and independence mirrors our own; its impending integration with other technologies reflects our global integration; and, as we look more closely into this looking glass (every bit as strange as the one Alice stepped through in Lewis Carroll's story), we begin to see an object which is more and more like ourselves: not an alien piece of hardware but an ever-present friend who reacts in familiar ways and with whom we feel at home.

Derrick de Kerckhove ('Notes for an Epistemology of Television') examines the way television is affecting our minds and bodies. He argues that the speed and directness with which television sends us images makes us 'feel' meaning rather than understand it through thought. Perhaps, he suggests, this is what makes watching television such a satisfying, almost infantile experience. It is challenging our current 'brainframe' – the way we process information – and is substituting its own.

In a separate contribution ('Roadside Romance: TV marries Computer on the Electronic Highway'), Derrick de Kerckhove examines the electronic superhighway and explores its implications for the future of television – and their combined effect on the economy. Digitisation has now replaced both money and the alphabet as the principal of way of representing information and resources. The convergence of technologies will expand the range of interactive video applications, such as video-conferencing, teleshopping, video-on-demand, and even virtual reality, each of which will have far-reaching social and economic consequences.

TV Design – Tomorrow and tomorrow and tomorrow

The other contributions look at television from the design point of view. As noted above, this book grew out of a series of design workshops and this practical origin is reflected in many of these writings.

In those workshops, young designers (all from Philips) explored ways of expressing ideas about the future of the medium in the design of the next generation of televisions. In doing so, they avoided the temptation to indulge in science fiction, accepting the confines of today's – or at least tomorrow morning's – technology. Their designs, focusing on a single portable format, are incredibly varied. In graphic form, accompanied by epigrammatic comments, they express their vision of the near future.

One significant aspect of the workshops was the context in which they were held. They were experimental, in that they brought together the respective skills and strengths, in many ways complementary, of a major industrial producer and small specialist design studios. This aspect of the project is discussed and placed in the perspective of twentieth-century international design trends by Andrea Branzi ('Crisis and Growth: Industrial Design and the Creative Tradition'). He argues that, over the past fifty years or more, economic and social crises have resulted in new models of growth, which, in turn, have brought with them new concepts of Design. He sees the present type of collaboration between multinationals and small studios, between the world of business and centres of design experimentation, as a response to the crisis of confidence following the collapse of East-West antagonism in the late nineteen-eighties, the subsequent dashing of hopes for a New Order in the early nineties, and the general anxiety surrounding environmental and economic issues.

La Bottega dell'Arte

A second significant aspect of the workshops was their format. In them, the designers worked as 'Pupils' under the guidance of older, more experienced colleagues – 'Masters'. The Masters set the theme for the workshop and provided practical assistance and encouragement. This particular relationship was reminiscent of that current in many artists' studios in Renaissance Florence. There, Master and Pupil together learned how to question, dare, imagine and feel, and then to communicate what they had found through meaningful form. For that reason, the workshops were given the name *La Bottega dell'Arte* – the Art Studio.

Here each Master provides an introduction to his workshop, sketching the themes and ideas that formed the focus of the Pupils' experimentation. Alessandro Mendini ('The Television as a Magic Lamp') emphasises the magical quality of television: its quality of allowing us to step into its world and become the protagonist – both watcher and watched – as well as its ability to dematerialise both itself and what it shows us. Andrea Branzi ('Towards a Post-Television Society') argues that television poses a problem not so much when it is on as when it is off, i.e., when it is a dead box cluttering up the home. He therefore focused the attention of his group of designers not on questions of design or form, but on the observation and analysis of reality as a source of innovative design ideas. Finally, in the introduction to my own workshop ('Into the Era of Soul'), I concentrate on the way in which the 'soul' of television – its meaningful elements – can satisfy a vast range of needs of individuals within the new polycentric domestic setting, taking over many functions formerly fulfilled by other objects and circumstances which, for one reason or another, we have banished from our lives.

Time-bound and Timeless

It was in this spirit of open-minded exploration that we approached the challenge of understanding more about television in the near future. What is the human experience of television? How *has* it changed us? How *will* it change us? What does it *mean*? How does it *feel*? What *is* it? What are *we* in relation to it? These are very much questions for our time. And although television itself is clearly time-bound, they are also eternal questions, touching on fundamental human concerns, drives and values – and, as such, infinitely fascinating.

The Magical Mirror

of Everyday Life

Francesco Morace

Dual Nature

More than any other product, television follows, interprets, and modifies the relationship that the individual maintains with the spaces and rhythms of life. At the same time, television possesses the magical capacity to become a mirror not only of contemporary everyday life but also of the profound transformation it is undergoing. It is at once object and 'meta-object'. While television features as an object in our everyday existence, that same existence is reflected back at us in the subject-matter of the medium. To try to understand the role, which this dual nature of television plays in our lives, we need to explore the interaction between technological and social developments and their joint impact on the individual.

From TV as Hearth to TV as Clock

For several decades, the television performed the function of a new hearth, a central point of attraction within the home, around which all family and individual life was reorganised. This reorganisation included the patterns of space and furnishing: the 'spatial' perspective that prevailed proved to be strongly centripetal and the object-television became the new domestic totem, the magnet that attracted and organised domestic relationships and hierarchies.

With the gradual dismemberment of the nuclear family and the increasing presence of more than one TV set in the home, television has assumed the role of marking time in people's lives.

Over the last decade, with the gradual dismemberment of the nuclear family and the appearance of virtual singles – individual members of the household with a high degree of autonomy – there has been a parallel proliferation of television sets in the home, with a gradual shift towards an experience of television that is less and less tied to a 'spatial' dimension and instead increasingly follows the logic of 'living time.'

The individual's experience of television has increasingly come to constitute the use made of a period of time, a programmed division of everyday life, and less and less the use of a shared family space. With growing frequency, people watch television alone and in a variety of places. It no longer represents a focus but a clock that marks out the individual's experience of time. This evolution in the relationship with the television as object is in reality the reflection of a broader change, and one which affects the whole of domestic life.

The traditional spatial typology, which divided the house up into specialised rooms with a single function, has given way to a typology of the environment based more on living time than on space. In every room of the house different things are done at different moments, and each room becomes a genuine living room. At certain points in everyday life, the activities traditionally tied to the living room (including watching television) are extended to other rooms, altering people's experience of them and their spatial structure. From this perspective, the television has become the *primum mobile* and is tending to turn into a 'transverse' piece of furniture (i.e., one that is present in every room of the house) and to make 'living time' a meaningful domestic experience.

Spatial Flexibility: Mobile TV

In the logic of living time, the organisation of domestic space is increasingly based on the concepts of flexibility and reversibility. It is not only in politics that the walls have come down; people now tend to avoid such divisions in their private lives as well, seeing them as elements that constrain and limit personal expression. The function once assigned to the structural elements of the house now tends to be performed by the archetypes of furnishing

Flexibility and mobility are fundamental requirements for today's home furnishings, and research into the development of cordless televisions is part of this trend.

(tables, armchairs, cupboards, bookcases), which are used more and more often to define boundaries, to create and distinguish zones in domestic space.

In the logic of flexibility, a special significance is assigned to those products that, besides replacing traditional structural elements, are themselves 'impermanent,' in the sense that they are modular, personalisable, sectional, and combinable; objects and products whose 'impermanence' does not derive from the idea of 'planned obsolescence' and 'disposability', cornerstones of the ephemeral consumption of the previous decade, but from their high potential for 'circulation' within the home. The impermanence implicit in this new organisation of domestic space does not concern the lifetime of products (which is tending to increase), but their flexibility, not their material aspect but their use.

Our relationship with the television set is also caught up in this phenomenon of transformation, and the new use to which the device is put often constitutes a cutting edge in this process through the development of three characteristics: miniaturisation, autonomy, and mobility. At present, the medium-sized television is still seen in terms of an essentially fixed object. This is the consequence both of its traditional role as a status symbol – to be displayed in the respectable drawing room, like the family silver – and of a number of powerful material constraints, such as its weight and the various connections required for it to function. Yet it seems evident that these characteristics no longer match the needs that are emerging from the patterns of daily life, which now require a more decentralised access to television.

As a result of this experience, therefore, the concept is emerging of a medium-sized television set that is flexible – i.e., mobile and autonomous – and which will generally be the second or third set in the house, after the totem television in the living room. Technically, this trend has been made feasible by the redesign of casing supports and the introduction of cordless operation. The work on supports is based on the idea of a movable television, a conceptually unitary object designed to be easily shifted from one part of the house to another. Another aspect of mobility is represented by the possibility of rotating the television and the screen around both the horizontal and the vertical axes, a feature that many manufacturers are now working on.

The development of cordless systems represents a step towards solving the problem of power supply and the cable connection with the antenna, factors which currently impose considerable limitations on the autonomy of the television set.

Demand for Interactivity and the Service TV

Another development linking our evolving home-life habits to the experience of the television as object is the growing demand for interactivity and the integration of domestic technologies into a single connective system running through the entire space of the home. In addition, the saturation of certain technology markets (such as that for personal computers) is a very important factor in the emergence of the growing demand for interconnection. Several fundamental sectors are moving towards a different model of consumption; and in this light, the need for people to be able to continue using the technologies already in their possession, and to expect compatibility, are considerations that become inescapable for producers.

Apart from these specific requirements, however, it is also necessary to take into account the tendency to no longer regard technologies as single products but rather as 'families', groups of products that are already compound and varied in nature today and that may expand to embrace even more elements in the future. Symptomatic of this is the television set, which is no longer regarded by people as a self-contained product, isolated from other technologies. At the very least it is associated with the video recorder, but in fact nowadays its 'family' often includes the hi-fi stereo, a signal decoder to decode signals from the satellite dish, a console for video games, a card for teletext and telecom video services, a keyboard, the hard disk of the computer, the CD-ROM player, and so on.

Today many new technologies form part of, and develop as, nodes in a network that has no central unit. Rather, all the units are linked together, sometimes performing the function of requesting information, at other times that of supplying services. Whatever the actual use made of this potential for connection, the fact remains that the experience of domestic technologies is evolving toward the image of the 'family', and that the ability to make connections strongly influences the image of individual products and the customer's decision to purchase them. In both real and symbolic terms (i.e., as a result of its 'historical' origins), the television set stands at the centre of this demand for interactivity, becoming the prime product of the entire system of connection.

Consequently, the concept of television as service provider assumes the demand for connections as one of the principal aspects of its identity, placing the emphasis on the television set's ability to link up and communicate with other categories of technology.

The service television is therefore a product that fits into the present panorama of technologies for the home, accepting a role that is also a supporting one for clusters of technologies and for the wide variety of uses to which these can be put. It is a television set that is leaving behind the era of one-way utilisation, turning as it does so into a device capable of accommodating a range of media and characterised by interactivity.

The idea of the TV set as an independent object is being replaced by the concept of television as service provider, with the set becoming only one element in a larger 'family' of devices.

TV and the Logic of the Sequence of Use

However, the most striking aspect of the change in our experience of television is the model of 'sequence of use' made possible by the remote control. For a decade now, our relationship with the television set as object and above all with the language of television has been completely transformed by the advent of the remote control. This device has intervened in four ways:
— by physically separating the product from the user, creating a spatial distance and eliminating any tactile contact with the television set;
— by modifying the processes of cognition and perception of the product, to the point where a television set without remote control is inconceivable, or is at least immediately regarded as obsolete;
— by increasing the complexity of the product's operation for the user, with the product not only having become more complicated in itself, but now being 'filtered' by another technological instrument, which is also complicated to use;
— and above all by making possible the selective and 'compulsive' viewing of television programmes, through the increasingly common phenomenon of 'zapping', or switching rapidly from one channel to another.

Within a short space of time, zapping has become the most powerful metaphor defining the identity of the post-industrial individual, who is also characterised by alternative and impulsive strategies of choice. Sociologists and psychologists have devoted rivers of ink to this phenomenon, and it will be sufficient for us here to point out that it has added a crucial new dimension to the relationship between the television and social reality.

The remote control has led to the formation of a fresh 'area of needs' in our relationship with the television set, covering both the traditional requirements of control and the new problems connected with the existence and use of a new object. But above all, it has turned the television into a continual source of stimuli and moving images, beginning a process of dematerialisation of the object-television that will probably reach its climax in the development of ultra-flat screens and, eventually, tele-walls. The disappearance of material support will mark the triumph of televisual language, which, completely liberated from the product, will then be seen as television form.

New Developments in the Experience of TV

The factors we have examined so far appear to be the most significant in the history of our experience of television to date. Let us now turn to consider some possible future developments in the use of television and in the way we perceive technology, quality, and service. We will do this by examining three concepts: the friendly television, the tactile television, and the expert television.

Technological Embarrassment and the Friendly TV

In these years of rapid technological progress, technology has spread faster than the consumer has been educated in how to use it, and its potentialities have remained largely underused.

One of the most significant effects of this gap has been a reaction of embarrassment, sometimes leading to rejection, with respect to excessively sophisticated technologies. The introduction of high-tech styling on a massive scale and the proliferation of functions and options 'for later connection', requiring the direct intervention of the user, may have been accepted as signs of modernity, but they have not yet been properly digested. In extreme cases, they are experienced as frustrating, as factors increasing the fragility of the product and engendering a sense of impotence in its user.

The concept of the friendly television becomes possible when changes in the hardware and software reduce that embarrassed response and turn mere options into real benefits. Technological innovation has to be proposed and developed in such a way that it can really be used by the 'average user'.

In this perspective, the user-friendly television becomes an everyday friend, an object with a 'humanity' of its own; no longer a cold technological product that can be difficult to use. Indeed, this trend has already been noted by a number of manufacturers, who are working on the concept of 'tactile television,' operated with a much simpler, reversible remote control or a 'mouse.'

Useful Value and the Tactile TV

Openness to innovation and experimentation is now increasingly seeking and finding a response in areas other than technology, such as the environment, the user's emotional associations, or fundamental quality.

Within the home, technological objects, especially those with markedly high-tech characteristics, are losing the central role they had acquired during the past decade, when, more than any other product, they symbolised sociocultural modernity and an advanced life-style. Today they form part of a domestic setting with a wide variety of characteristics, camouflaged among a multitude of signs that are not technological, but rather have a high

Manufacturers are trying to compensate for the increased complexity which has resulted from new technology by giving their sets 'friendly' controls, endowed with familiar and emotional qualities.

In the Tactile TV, the form of the set loses its high-tech connotations, to fit smoothly into a fluid and heterogeneous domestic setting.

emotional, almost tactile, content. In line with this trend, the concept of tactile television means abandoning the markedly high-tech connotation now typical of the vast majority of products on the market: not the sacrifice of their technological content, which is, of course, indispensable, but a move away from the codified forms, materials, and stylistic features of high-tech aesthetics.

In the rapidly changing domestic environment and value system, technologies are tending to lose some of their symbolic and communicative value and are shifting towards value in use. The television set as product is now ceasing to be used as an 'identifying' item of property. Instead, it is increasingly being camouflaged so as to merge into the altered home landscape. In that new setting, it will have to change its morphology and accept a role in which its status as an object depends purely on the functions it offers and the use to which it is put. In this sense, the television set will truly become a carrier and interpreter of the information flow, no longer a passive object but an active participant in communication, capable of creating empathy and relationships.

Demand for Quality and the Expert TV

The demand for quality, now generalised and constantly growing, is taking on specific characteristics in relation to technological products, and to television sets in particular. The past decade saw the introduction of a number of new technologies which have had a powerful impact on everyday life at home and at work. Microelectronics has resulted in the development of completely new categories of products (in the field of information processing, for instance), and in the transformation of already existing products, both in the way we view them and in the way we interact with them. With incredible rapidity, the market has proposed and imposed products like the personal computer, the fax, and the cellular phone, items which the ordinary consumer had not experienced or even heard of before.

The current demand for quality in these products not only reflects a generic maturity on the part of the consumer, it also indicates the latter's deeper understanding and sharper critical powers with respect to what is on offer, abilities gained and refined through experience and experimentation over the past few years.

In the case of television, the demand for quality relates directly to the quality of the medium's programme content, i.e., quality during use. This also implies, alongside the traditional requirements of durability and functionality, a demand for high standards of performance.

The concept of expert television tackles the question of performance by distinguishing basic functions from more specialised ones. The basic functions are those dealing with the visual and sound qualities of the product. For optimal quality of use, these must be of a high standard. The specialised functions are those associated with the current trend towards selective television 'consumption'. Zapping and choosing programmes in advance encourages a high level of consumption and the restriction of interest to certain types of programmes. Developing further in the same direction, expert television offers specialised functions within the various televisual genres (rock music, sport, drama, news, etc.). Its proponents see it as a way of allowing the viewer to enjoy the preferred genre to the full by, for example, incorporating sophisticated techniques for manipulating the image. In this way, the quality offered will go beyond the product itself to affect directly not only what it provides but also all the funtions it is increasingly being asked to perform.

Alessandro Mendini

work

The Television as a Magic Lamp shop

19

Design Values

I consider the workshop held with a group of young Philips designers as a special experience. The direct relationship between the project of an individual designer (such as myself) and a colossal industrial structure (such as Philips) was mediated, shaped and organised by the young in-house design group, with an excellent combination of the requirements of both parties. The experimental and didactic nature of the 'television project' allowed us to go into the problems freely and in depth, not only in terms of product design but also in relation to the psychological aspects of this object, which represents the visual communication and propensity for sensation of our age.

Taking for granted its technical and functional validity, a design object nowadays only becomes fascinating and significant if it is able to assume sympathetic mental, spiritual and ritual values. The television is a container for an infinite number of messages, but its role is neutral. When it is switched off, it is not only an unlit lamp, but an ill-matched obstacle amongst the other pieces of furniture; when it is switched on, it is a doubtful item of household electrical equipment, associated with the typical image of functional electronics.

Feeling of Magic

In the workshop held in my offices in Milan, the young Philips designers were completely free to apply their individual expression. Nevertheless, I asked them to ensure that their projects included the spiritual and ritual *quid* or essence which would make the presence of the object interesting when switched off and expressive when switched on. I feel that the outcome was altogether positive. Since small, portable televisions were involved, we considered that the surroundings should not be taken into account, and concentrated on the form of the televisions as objects, and the possibility of putting them in any room and on any piece of furniture, or even on the ground.

Free choice of forms, materials, colours and finishes, even if startling, gave rise to the creation of a small series of objects which, although they varied greatly, all had in common the underlying feeling of magic which we were seeking.

The Object Television

The television is a household electrical appliance, a means of watching at home the images of entertainments and events which have taken place or are taking place elsewhere. It is a device which brings entertainment, news and culture into our homes. As such it is one of the most unsettling objects of modern society. Initially, it stood in the sitting room like a miniature cinema, replacing the hearth as the focus of family life. Now, the increased choice of channels and our familiarity with the medium have given rise to the concept of small individual televisions. This leads on to the idyllic concept of rooms with all four walls acting as television screens, and ultimately even the complete lack of a set, with the screen being projected in atmospheric particles.

Space and Size

The cult of functional architecture and industrial design has left its mark on concepts of size and geometric space. Previously, three-dimensional space was the basic element in the creation of an object, including a television, but now things have changed. Other values and aspects of the design problem have come to the fore in the creation of the form of certain objects. Many 'external' disciplines, which have nothing to do directly with the object or with size, are making considerable innovations, and geometric space is no longer felt to be essential.

New Design

The 'Postmodern' world is breaking down subject barriers in order to set the world's future scene. New design infiltrates the divides between subjects such as anthropology, art, psychology, religion, cinema and so on. Thus, the cinema gives precedence to entirely non-material space, as opposed to a typical space containing a physical structure; and the idea of transferring this notion to a 'material' object is full of promise. Similarly, fashion, which gives precedence to space and time, involves an idea of obsolescence of images which is entirely different from that conceived in design.

For the purposes of the present project, more intriguing still is the structure of the television image, since both linguistically and stylistically, television creates systems of altogether new colours; it transforms the world into a type of texture, into a highly visual pointillism. It has the same kind of value as architecture – in other words, that of turning the spectator himself into the show, and of enabling him to get inside the screen and the location in order to become a protagonist.

Yet even as an object, the television can be something ultramodern if it can manage to dispense with its physical essence and become a virtual surface which is entirely subject to the options of the person using it. Television is not merely a form of entertainment. It is, rather, a type of total substitute for the reality, the geometry and the space of an area. Indeed, at a certain point, a whole architectural world can be

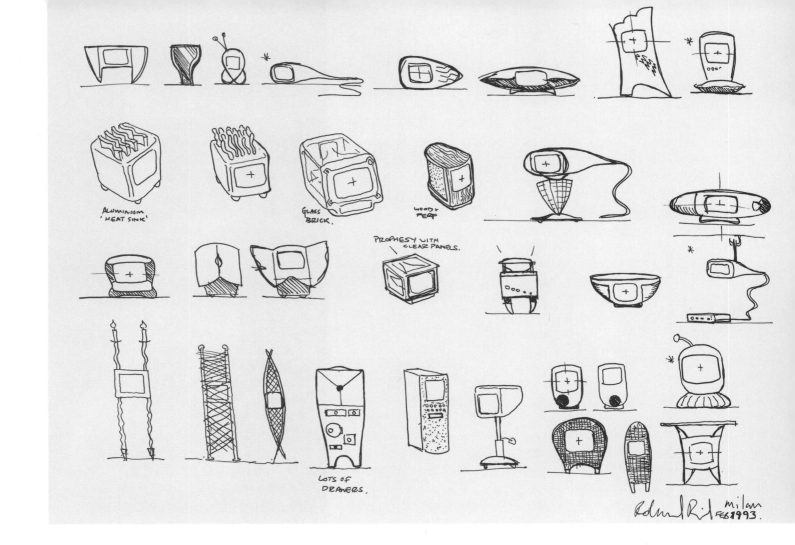

PHILIPS
WORKSHOP
A.M.
93

transformed into television. The physical essence of the world is transposed conceptually into this non-material form, and buildings as such lose all substance. This dematerialisation of objects is not something from the realms of science fiction, but is a step towards a potential earthly nirvana, where man loses his desire for things physical, and is surrounded only by simulated nature, where tangible objects no longer exist.

On track for fun

A bridge too low? Just adjust the legs. Then even

toy trains will run on time. If we hurry, we can

catch the next express to Anywhere...

I had my doubts about following Alessandro Mendini's advice and shortening the legs of my set. I felt sure this would disrupt the balance between body and legs. But the result amazed me: a simple, straightforward design with a definite personality. Merely by reinterpreting the proportions, a simple, characterless design had been transformed into one which had taken on an almost timeless character. Suddenly I understood what he had been trying to tell me.

Francis Chu

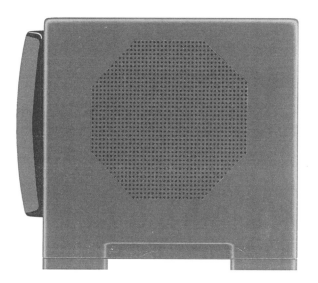

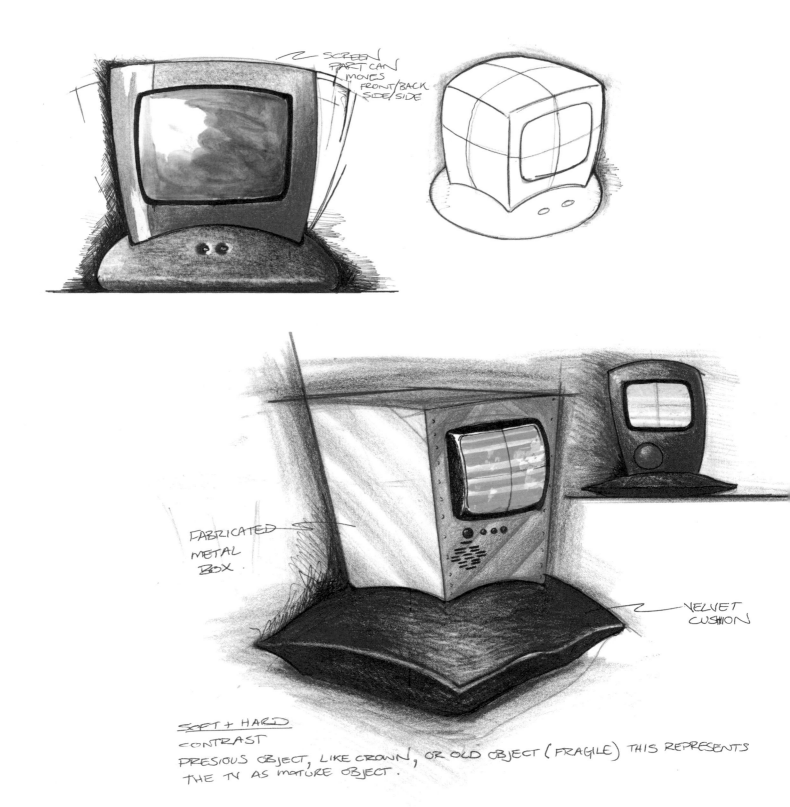

SCREEN PART CAN MOVES FRONT/BACK SIDE/SIDE

FABRICATED METAL BOX.

VELVET CUSHION

SOFT + HARD CONTRAST
PRESIOUS OBJECT, LIKE CROWN, OR OLD OBJECT (FRAGILE) THIS REPRESENTS
THE TV AS mature OBJECT.

Guitar Man

Telelessons encourage a budding star to rival his

idol. Afterwards, in cushioned comfort, hard work

is rewarded with an inspiring concert in hi-fi sound

and perfect image.

Television can mean anything to anyone. Far from being an inert, neutral box, the set can a vehicle for good or evil. To counter its inherent dangers, why not make it something that requires more active input rather than less? Televiewing would then no longer be a passive act but a conscious one, like the act of will required to open a book and start reading.

Roland Bird

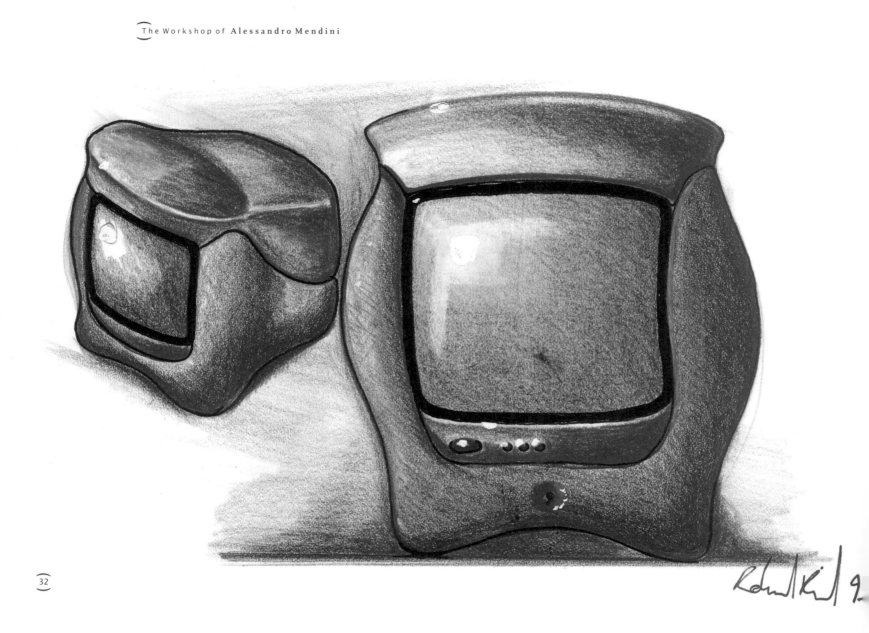

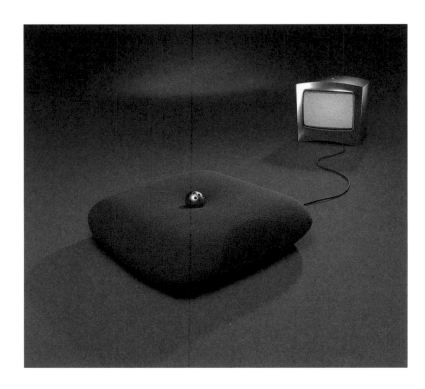

Here's looking at you, kid

When choosing make-up from the TV, you can always play it again. Screen model and mirror image blend into reality. Turn the set over when you're done: Bogie's waiting...

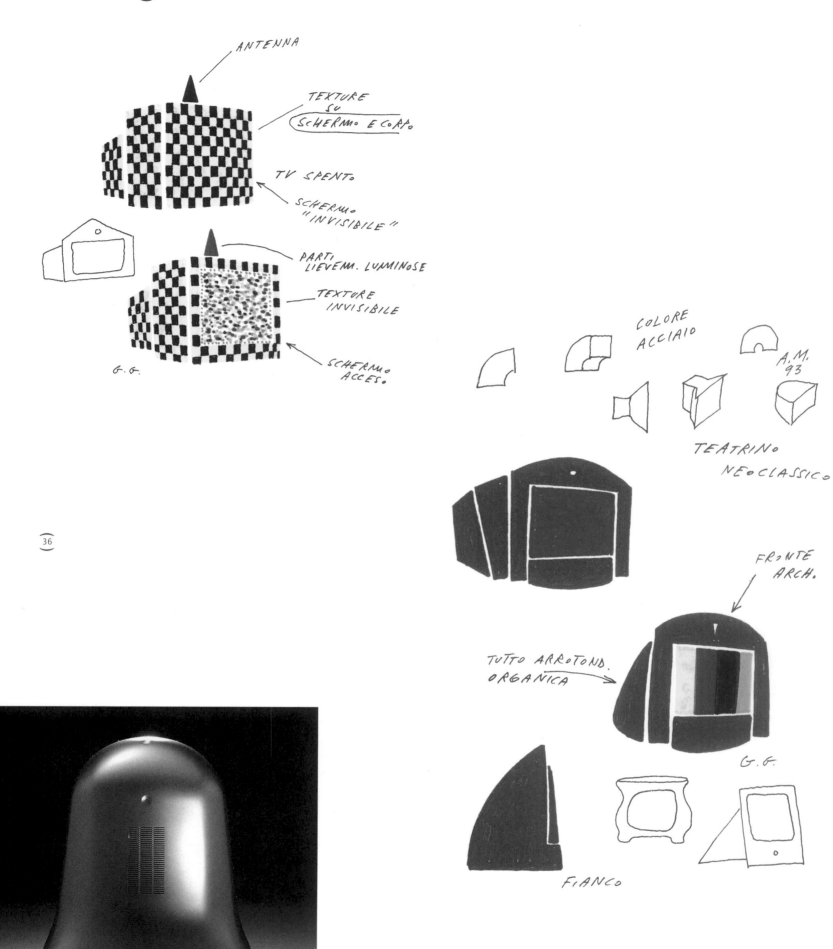

ANTENNA

TEXTURE
SU
SCHERMO E CORPO

TV SPENTO

SCHERMO
"INVISIBILE"

PARTI
LIEVEM. LUMINOSE

TEXTURE
INVISIBILE

SCHERMO
ACCESO

G.G.

36

COLORE
ACCIAIO

A.M.
93

TEATRINO
NEOCLASSICO

FRONTE
ARCH.

TUTTO ARROTOND.
ORGANICA

G.G.

FIANCO

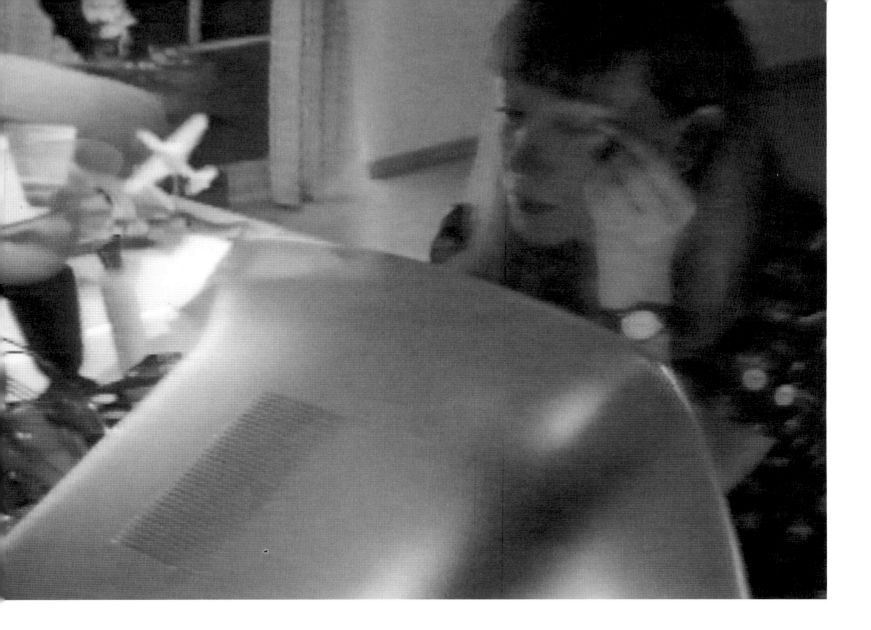

Magic-carpet ride

Holiday dreams for two become reality as we view
resorts we could visit. Controls in the carpet let us
book and pay. Can't wait to just fly away!

From the first day, I realised that this
workshop presented us with a rare
opportunity: a chance to express our
feelings about some of the social
problems of our time and even to
suggest a possible solution to some
of them through the medium of
design.

Benny Leong

OBJECT ON TOP
NOT WELCOME

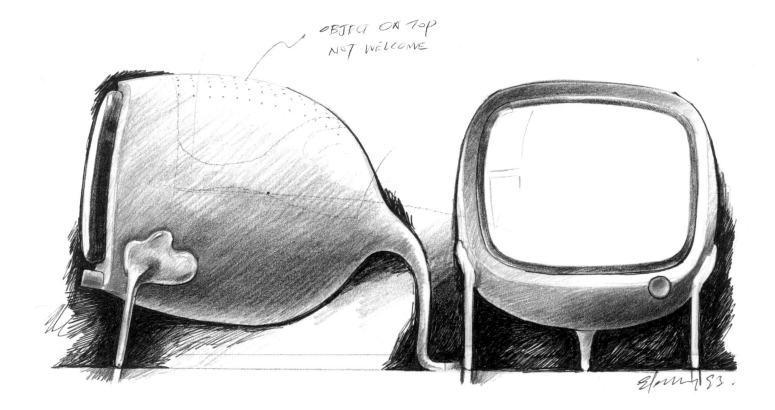

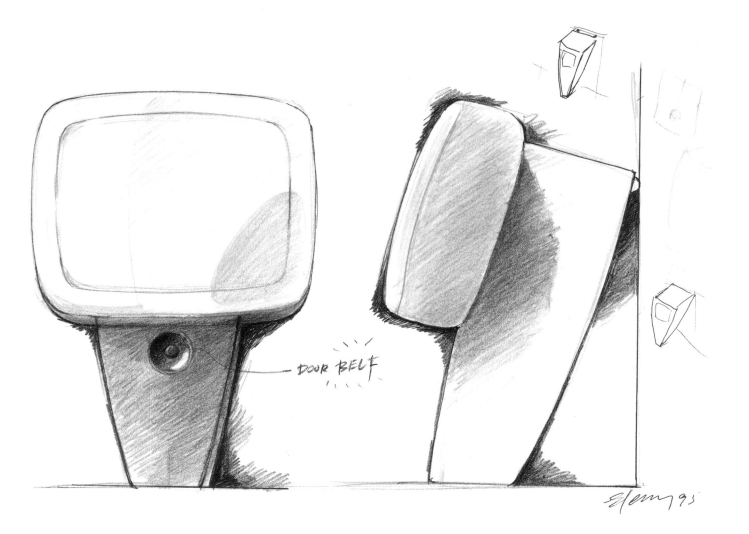

DOOR BELF

My designs have a triple focus: involvement
and integration (design with soul), mood
and feeling (playful design) and
individuality and stimulation (a strong
statement).

Benny Leong

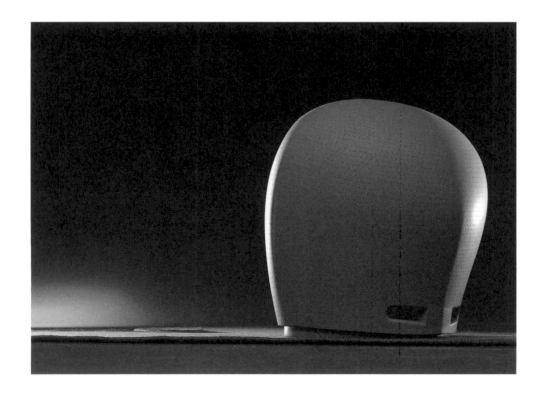

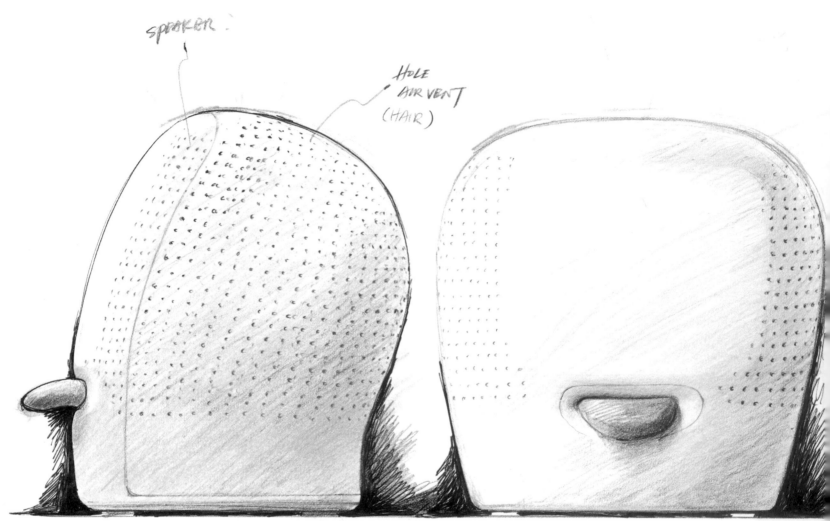

SPEAKER

HOLE
AIR VENT
(HAIR)

'Original', 'simple' and 'pure': to each
member of the group these words of
Alessandro Mendini may have meant
something different. But an important
part of our inspiration would be
drawn from the Master's non-verbal
statements – his rough design
sketches.

Benny Leong

VALCO

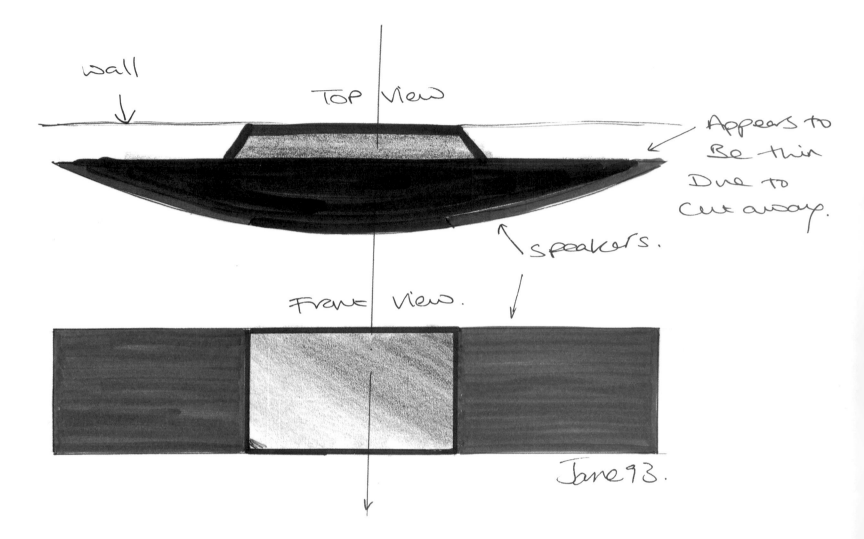

wall

TOP View

Appears to
Be thin
Due to
Cut away.

speakers.

Front View.

June 93.

Mrs Bovary

A rare evening together: reading under the telelamp, looking round the telemall. But there's bad news for Mr B.: the Dow's down. While he rushes over to the office Mrs B. snuggles under... with a friend.

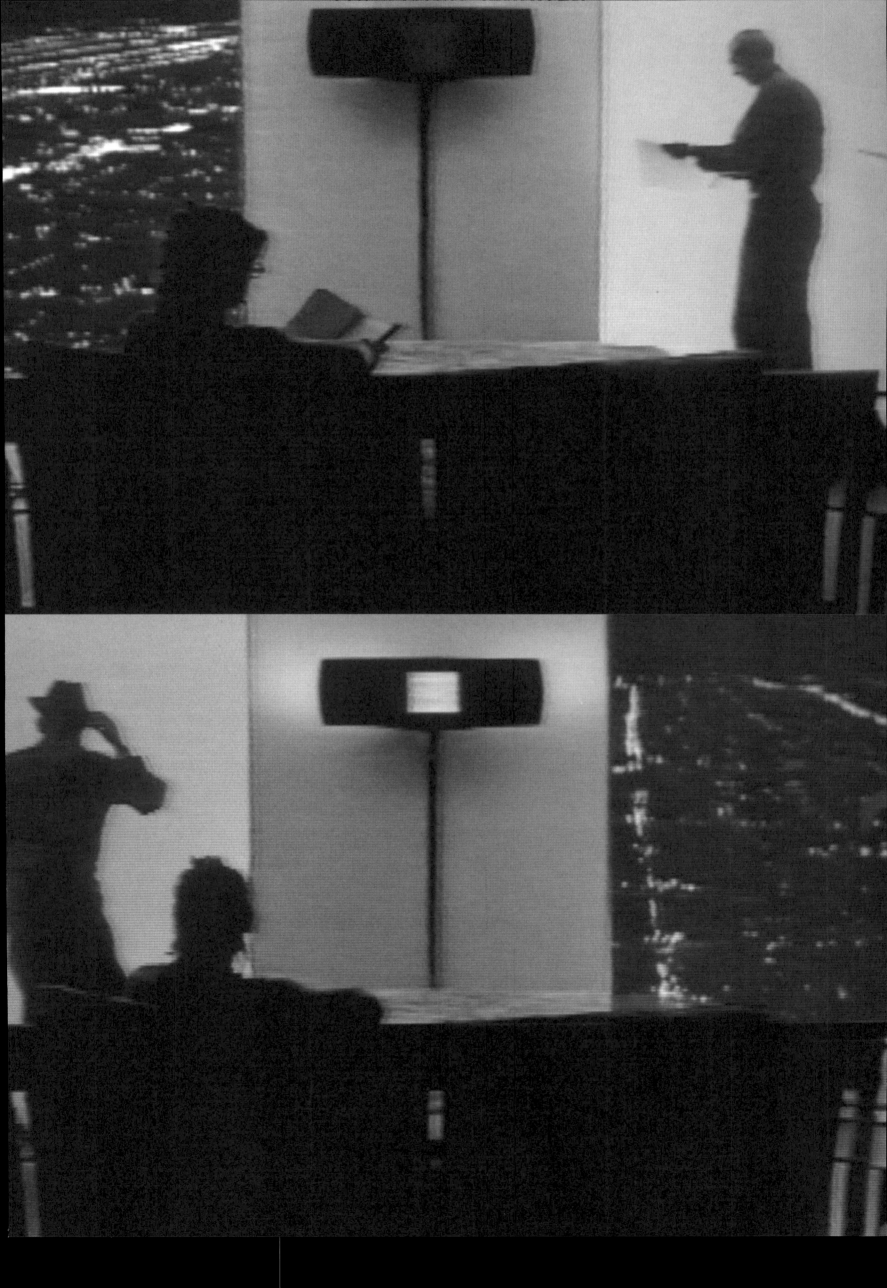

Many domestic appliances were once displayed with pride. Now, in our clutter-free interiors, they are tucked out of sight. Soon we may also want to hide the television, or to have it merge into the background. To explore these two subtle extremes, I chose strong, geometric pieces of furniture as the basis of my designs.

Jane Worthington

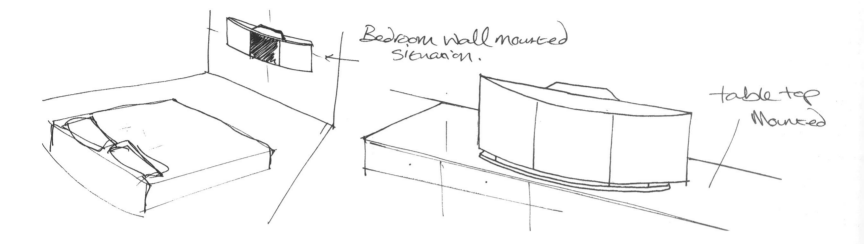

Bedroom wall mounted
situation.

table top
Mounted

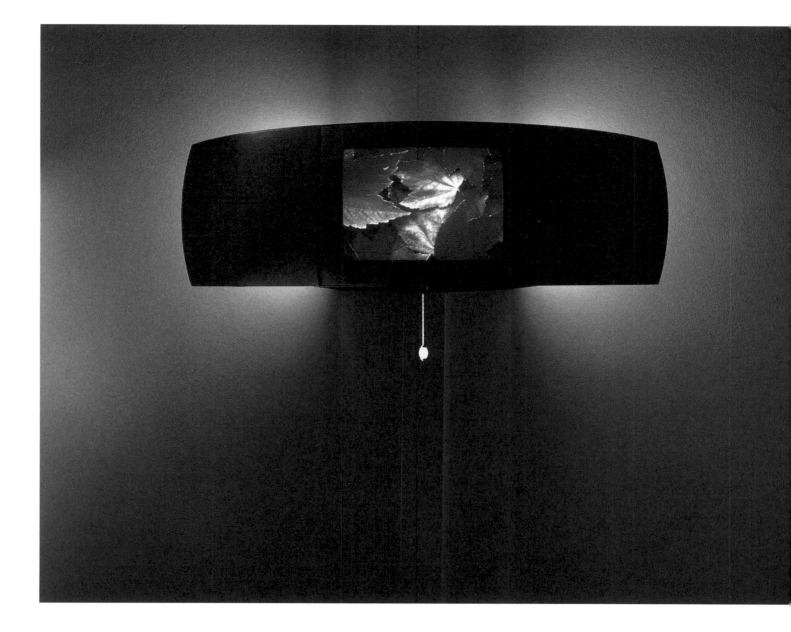

Television evolved as a generic
product, ignoring all individual
factors such as social group,
geographic origin, age or gender –
a mass market product.
We are beginning to understand that
there is more. But how can we bring
about change?

Jane Worthington

Notes for an

Epistemology of

Television

Derrick de Kerckhove

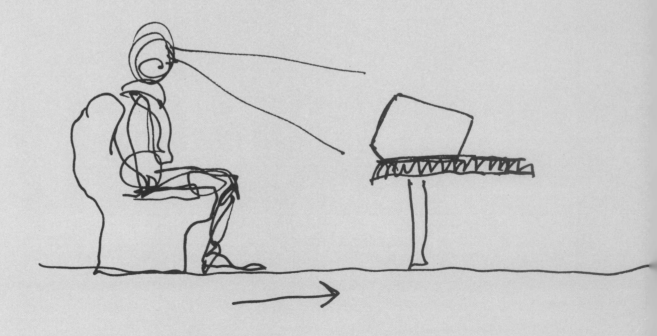

Attractive Hypnotist

Says Woody Allen to Diane Keaton, driving in a taxi in *Manhattan*: "You're so beautiful, I can hardly keep my eyes on the meter". TV is more powerful than a taximeter; you can't keep your eyes off it. Why is it so difficult, just as we are about to declare our passion to someone, to prevent ourselves from watching TV if the set is turned on in the background? Because television is *hypnotically* involving: any movement on the screen attracts our attention almost as automatically as if someone had just touched us accidentally. Our eyes are dragged to the set like iron to a magnet.

Orienting and Defensive Responses

Understanding our television culture depends upon understanding why and how television fascinates us beyond our conscious control. Images on video are being closely watched and followed all the time by my neuromuscular system, even if my mind occasionally wanders or dozes off. The reason why that cannot be helped is that, because of antediluvian biological programming, the autonomic nervous systems of all higher mammals is trained to respond to any and every perceptible change in their environment that might be relevant to their survival. We are indeed conditioned by our autonomic nervous system to respond involuntarily to any kind of stimulation, whether internal or external, with either what in clinical psychophysiology is called the Orienting Response (OR), which alerts our attention towards the stimulus, or the Defensive Response (DR), which makes us recoil from the stimulus.

Now, you might ask, just what is so relevant to our survival in the standard television fare? Not much in terms of content, but TV's principal action, as Marshall McLuhan observed, does not happen at the level of content but at that of the medium itself, that is, at the level of the flickering light of the electron beam scanner. The basic units of TV effects are the changes and cuts in the shows which provoke continuous ORs, alerting attention without necessarily satisfying it. In life, we get used to stimuli even as we get to know them: either we recognise them and deal with them appropriately or, with new, unknown stimuli, we develop a quick strategy to deal with them, and we add them to our repertory of experience. A completed response to a stimulus is called a closure. In life, most stimuli evoke an OR, call for a closure and receive it; then we are done with it. With television, we are never done with the initial stimulus: TV provokes rapid successions of ORs without allowing time for closure.

The 'Collapse of the Interval' between Stimulus and Response

In a paper on cognitive responses to television, German media theorist, Hertha Sturm made an important observation about how, when we watch television, we are denied the time necessary to integrate the information on a conscious basis: "Rapidly changing presentations impair verbalisation. Among these are uninterpreted changes in viewing angle, unpredictable flip-flops from picture to text or from text to picture. When confronted with rapidly changing presentations and speeded-up action, the viewer is literally driven from image to image. This demands constantly new and unexpected adaptation to perceptual stimulation. As a result, the viewer is no longer able to 'keep up' and ceases to internally label. When this occurs, we found, the individual acts and reacts with heightened physiological arousal, which in turn results in a reduction in comprehension. The viewer becomes, so to speak, a victim of an external force, of rapid audio-visual sequencing."[1]

1. H. Sturm, 'Perception and television: The missing half-second', *The Work of Hertha Sturm*, edited and translated from German by Gertrude J. Robinson, Working Papers in Communications (Montreal: McGill University, 1988), p.39.

53

The suggestion is that television leaves us little if any time at all to reflect on what we are watching. Hertha Sturm claims that it takes the mind at least half a second to provide proper closure to complex stimuli. She says TV denies it to the spectator and she calls that 'the missing half-second syndrome'.

Jolts Per Minute (JPMs) and the 'Missing Half-Second'

The automatic reflex activity of our ORs to television is all the more pressing since, unlike what happens with cinema screens, the light coming from the video screen does not bounce back from it into our eyes. It comes right at us through the screen, challenging us to respond. Sturm is probably correct in suggesting implicitly that television programming is deliberately geared to prevent our verbalised responses so as to make us better victims of unimpeded advertising.

We hear a lot of uninspired moralising about that. In a lighter vein, Toronto media critic Morris Wolfe created the concept of 'Jolts Per Minute' – or JPMs as they are now called – to describe how TV shows hit us. The notion behind JPMs is that it takes so many electronic cuts and jars are needed to prevent the viewer from falling asleep or switching channels. TV must zap the zapper before he or she zaps the channel. JPMs which keep the attention alive may also prevent cognitive closure.

Sub-Muscularisation and 'Felt Meaning'

However, in spite of what the self-appointed moralists have to say, this is not necessarily a bad thing. One effect of the collapse of the interval is that, just in order to make sense of the rapid succession of images reaching us from the screen, we have to somehow 'emulate' the action with our bodies. We do that just like children who often help their understanding of new or difficult concepts by 'going through the motion'. We follow the TV action with our body, and even imitate the occasional facial expression to better interpret it. This is what I call the 'sub-muscularisation effect', by analogy with the well-known 'sub-vocalisation' strategy adopted by slow readers to help them understand what they are reading. Sub-muscularisation is the interpretation of motion and action by a sort of sensorimotor mimicry involving the whole body in attention. I suggest that we interpret gestures, postures and expressions on TV with a kind of sub-muscular response, expressed in muscle tone and stress factors. Thus, 'television sense' is not the same as 'book sense'; it is closer to what the American psychologist and philosopher Eugene T. Gendlin calls 'felt meaning'.

2. Eugene T. Gendlin, *Experience and the Creation of Meaning*, New York, Free Press, 1964, p.27.

Gendlin defines felt meaning as "the equivalent of hundreds of thousands of cognitive operations done in a split second by the body"[2] in response to stimuli. Felt meaning could be said to be a product of sub-muscularisation. Indeed, as we experience events in our immediate surroundings, we store their relevant effects in various ways within our neuromuscular system. That is precisely what the Montreal-based clinical psychologist Hans Selye called 'stress'.

Although we know that we stop breathing when we are anxious, or that we blush when we are put to even mild shame, we are not usually aware of other physical events happening in our bodies which make up our global response to people and situations. Felt meaning does not rise to the level of consciousness, at least not directly, but, in the background, it regulates and conditions our overall response to everyday matters. Felt meaning precedes logic and may be much more comprehensive than thought. Thus the deeper effect of television might occur at the level of felt meaning rather than at the conscious level which, according to various theorists, is not given much chance to respond. TV might well engage us not only to imitate but to interpret images with physical responses. Television evokes Orienting Responses and sorts them out in stress points which are woven into the fabric of our neuromuscular system. That may be the source of McLuhan's rather cryptic intuition that television is 'tactile'.

The Pleasure of Television

Television's invitation to 'think with one's body' may be one of the reasons why watching television is experienced as satisfying. Another possibile explanation is that television evokes some of the most powerful infantile associations of our earliest gropings towards consciousness. Just as the refreshing pleasure of rhythm is said to come from our early association of our mother's heartbeat with the comfort of the womb, the pleasure generated by TV, irrespective of content, may come from the explicitness of a natural but unsuspected response to the combination of sound, image and gesture. Neurobiology has discovered that we are not born fully equipped with all our sensory inputs fully functioning; part of our neurophysiological development, and especially sensory correlations, occur after birth through exposure to experience.

Babies experience joy at hitting their spoons against their table because they see, feel and hear simultaneously the resulting sensation. The joy may come from the reinforcement of our first synaptic correlations when we begin to make sense, as infants, of the combined perceptions of sight, sound and touch. This 'emotion of sensory coordination' may go a long way to explain why children are so fascinated by TV. They can observe there the endless synchronicity of sensory inputs in focused imagery. The same explanation might apply to the joy they find in cartoons, where the correlation of sensory inputs is often emphasised to the detriment of visual definition. In that case, for adults, TV would feed a powerful infantile memory.

"Grazing and Zapping are the Way We Attend to Everything"

This is how social critic Michael Ignatieff condemns television. He is probably reflecting the opinion of many Canadians when he claims that TV is turning us into a "clever but shallow culture". It is easy, not to say facile, to heap blame on television. Often without much more than a hunch to go on, many thoughtful people attribute to television some major social evils, accusing it of desensitising us and promoting violence (including rape, murder and suicide), weakening both identity and community, reducing attention span, concentration, imagination and memory skills, developing cynical apathy, destroying civic values and supporting the urge for instant gratification. Recently, a group of committed citizens in Vancouver felt so strongly about the dangers of television addiction that they commissioned and paid for a series of TV ads to discourage people from watching it ("This sight is bad for you; stop looking right now").

Such rampant hostility towards television can be explained in many ways. However, only a few critics, including, perhaps, Jerry Mander, George Gerbner, Joshua Meyrowitz, Neil Postman and certainly McLuhan, have begun to understand the deeper message of the medium: TV is challenging our previously dominant brainframe and is trying to substitute its own, the videoframe, even as it threatens the sacrosanct autonomy we have acquired through reading and writing.

55

You Don't Watch TV, TV Watches You

There is not much that is 'innocent' about the way we use our eyes. Jean-Marie Pradier of the University of Paris observed that places such as theatres and red-light districts are 'free-viewing' areas, where one is allowed to be a voyeur.[3]

Is television such a free-viewing area? The relevance of this question was brought home to me by a recent video art installation. In *Face to Face*, Mit Mitropoulos had two participants sit back to back and converse with each other's images recorded in real time on closed-circuit video monitors. Although it is deceptively simple, the experience is unforgettable. Irrespective of whether I did or did not know my partner beforehand, and of whether it was a man, a woman or a child, I felt as if there were none of the usual bars against staring at someone right in the face. You could almost pick your nose in the context of this new electronic intimacy. True, I measured for the first time the extent to which we are terrified of each other's faces in ordinary live contact, but what struck me even more was that, for the last thirty years, we have unwittingly been watching our TV personalities without a trace of shyness. TV voyeurism is the 'uncensored gaze'. Television provides an unfettered free-viewing area.

Or so it seems. The deep involvement required by screen watching, and the fact that most of the responses of our body escape the control of our mind in responding to the flickering beam, bears witness to the changing power relationship between consumer and producer. While we read, we scan books, we are in control; but when we watch TV, it is the TV scanner that 'reads' us. Our retinas are the direct object of the electron beam; hence, we are being scanned. When scanning meets glancing and makes eye-contact between man and machine, the machine's glance is the more powerful of the two. In front of the television set, our defences are down; we are more vulnerable and we are all the more susceptible to multisensory seduction. Thus, the real meaning of 'prime time' could be 'priming time', that is, the best time to prime the mind of the television spectator. And, as the New York advertising executive and TV critic Tony Schwartz has suggested, "TV is not a window on the world, it's a window on the consumer."[4]

'Glancing' versus 'Scanning'

How does the television image reach our retina? Herbert Krugman has suggested that children brought up in front of the television do not look at things or even books in the normal way. Instead of using their eyes sequentially to see one thing at a time and sort and store information in succession, Krugman suggests that they take 'quick looks': "Television teaches the young child to 'learn to learn' in a very special manner, ... even before he has ever looked at a book. So the child learns to learn by quick looks. Later, if the child is in a society where reading is required, he confronts the new 'learn to learn' medium with the habit he has picked up earlier from TV. He tries to comprehend print via quick looks. It doesn't work. Learning to read is difficult, hard – and this comes as a surprise, an intolerable one in many cases."[5]

If Krugman's hypothesis is correct, the consequence is that our information-processing strategies could be quite different before and after the TV era.

It appears that, when young children read, they do not scan the text with the type of saccadic eye movements that are characteristic of the trained reader, but instead literally 'throw their eyes' on the page, as if they were transferring their visual strategy from the TV screen to the text. They seem to 'glance' at things, seizing the 'whole picture' at once,

3. Jean-Marie Pradier, 'Toward a biological theory of the body in performance', *New Theatre Quarterly*, February 1990, p.89.

4. Tony Schwartz, *Media, the Second God* (Garden City: Anchor Books, 1983).

5. Herbert E. Krugman, 'Memory without recall, exposure without perception', *Journal of Advertising Research*, Vol. 7, no.4, August 1977, p.8.

looking at it several times as if they were completing and compiling bits and pieces of text to make sense of it. This may have an important cognitive impact: instead of scanning the text to create and store images, children who watch TV must quickly generalise from loosely connected fragments and reconstitute the object of thought. This is very different from labelling objects and stringing them together in coherent sentences that, in turn, provide unified inner visions.

With print, we have to go through elaborate constructions to achieve a stable image. No wonder we need training to learn to read, not only before we can put letters together, but even after, when we go to school to learn to really get the maximum meaning from the text. Nobody needs any instruction to watch TV. With TV, we are constantly rebuilding images which are complete neither on the screen nor in our mind at first. This is a very exciting and dynamic process which bears some of the characteristics of the way our nervous system works. TV cuts up information, news, entertainment and advertising into minimal and often unconnected segments, jamming in as much information as possible in the shortest time. We take suggestions and complete the picture. Our mind works by instant generalisations from a few cues. However, that does not imply that we 'make sense' in the ordinary way, only that we 'make images'. Making sense by applying labels is another thing altogether, something which does not seem to be essential in television watching.

Editing versus Modulating

Television, patterned along the lines of film, has adopted editing as its norm. But because its technical principle is an electromagnetic pulse, its condition is in fact closer to music than to photography; as a completely electronic device, television, like the telegraph, the telephone, and radio, is a modulator. With television, the forceful and rapid manipulation of our neurophysiological responses (our felt-meaning system) goes well beyond the step-by-step, frame-by-frame, image-by-image type of editing used in film. It is so rapid, so continuous and so forceful that it is more like a magnetic modulation of our sensibility. Television modulates our sensibility, our emotions and our imagination in a way comparable to the power of music; that is why video-rock is a natural television creature, like televangelism, advertising and talk shows.

'Feel-good TV'

This is another aspect of the mysteriously 'tactile' dimension that McLuhan attributed to television. When he suggested in later books that "the medium is the massage", making fun of his own celebrated aphorism, what he meant was that television 'caresses' us and rubs its meaning under our skin.

TV favours repetition over analysis, myths over facts. It firebrands its icons on our psyche as if they were the walls of our cities. Homogenisation spreads like wildfire via TV, since nobody wants to be caught out of style. TV sounds, colours and shapes are the sensory expressions of our collective sensibility. But TV regimentation of our sensibility takes other forms too, such as track-laughter and applause, or, on a subtler level, electronic polling. Most information that appears on TV news and documentaries is 'pre-digested' and proposed in stereotypical instant narratives for a quick grab (like 'fast food'). TV has virtually created a 'mass' culture, removing the bearings of private reflection and self-building. The overnight success of Trivial Pursuit, a parlour game invented and

57

distributed during the early eighties, essentially a review of TV lore, seems to indicate that most of us share approximately the same body of trivia. In all this, TV may very well be doing our thinking for us, or at least, that part of our thinking that requires that we be both comprehensive and fast. Without necessarily always putting itself in the place of our own thoughts, the television screen may be the port of entry for our individual participation in a permanently on-going collective rumination.

TV Screens, Computer Screens and Other Videobrain Frames

Perhaps the most important unknown psychological effect of television is that it tends to *externalise* both the program and the frame of our personal information-processing system. In the psychological set-up created by literacy, the program and the frame are inside the mind. The program – or structuring code – is the alphabet, inside as a result of learning, and affecting in a semi-permanent way the organisation of our visual system. The frame is our mental space, an internalised simulation based on our normal perception of external time and space.

With television, both the program and the frame are outside. The programming is clearly done from the outside in, in many more senses than the obvious one. Even our time is minutely programmed by the TV hour. The frame, of course is the TV screen itself. Being two-dimensional, it eliminates perspective instantly. McLuhan observed that, quite literally, there cannot be a point-of-view in front of a TV. Besides the fact that, as with any film or video medium, the point-of-view is inescapably provided by the camera, there is also the impossibility of changing the angle of vision in front of a small two-dimensional screen. The TV screen is also a rigorously prescriptive frame, because all at once it frames the dimensions of whatever there is to look at, focuses the eyes and the attention of the spectator upon its small universally 3/4 ratio area, and conditions absolutely the way the information is processed and delivered.

The Epistemology of Electricity

Our rapid adoption of personal computers can be understood as the necessary step of individuation in the video media penetration of the social body. We might compare this with the beginnings of literacy. Soon after writing first appeared on the walls of the city, lighter writing materials became available which allowed for individual access – and the subsequent, ensuing and consequent development of democracy. What we are witnessing, of course, is a transition from the previous literate era dominated by books to a new human shape, a new mind, based on electronic communication. This transition is not quite complete yet. We are still developing technologies and methods to extend and amplify our most subtle and complex human qualities. Just as the computer can be better understood as a system of 'amplified' rather than 'artificial' intelligence, so virtual reality, by translating sight, sound, and touch in electronic data for any kind of display, becomes a kind of 'amplified imagination'.

By the same token, TV is a system of 'amplified memory'. As such, it deserves our attention and even our respect. Within the range of simulations allowed by electronic extensions of our bodies and minds, television and video do what the other media are not meant to do, which is to address, select, record, and play back reality in real time. TV is, like the telephone and radio, an extension of our sensory system. It is our first true and so far best collective information-processing device. Perhaps the most important benefit of television to mankind has been to provide a ubiquitous forum of instant information processing for large numbers of people and an area of interface where critical issues concerning world peace and security, and now issues of environmental control and North-South relationships can be examined and understood in context by everyone on a day-to-day basis. That which we needlessly fear to lose at one level, our private point of view on any issue, is regained at another level, one much more important for world affairs, but now in the form of a collective bargaining with reality.

This is an abridged version of an article which appeared under the title 'Videobrain',
in *Brainframes, Technology, the Mind and Business* (Utrecht: Bosch and Keuning, 1991)

Andrea Branzi

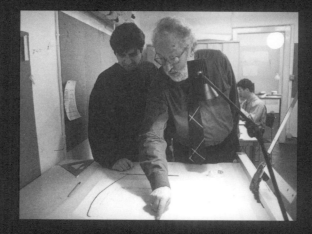

work

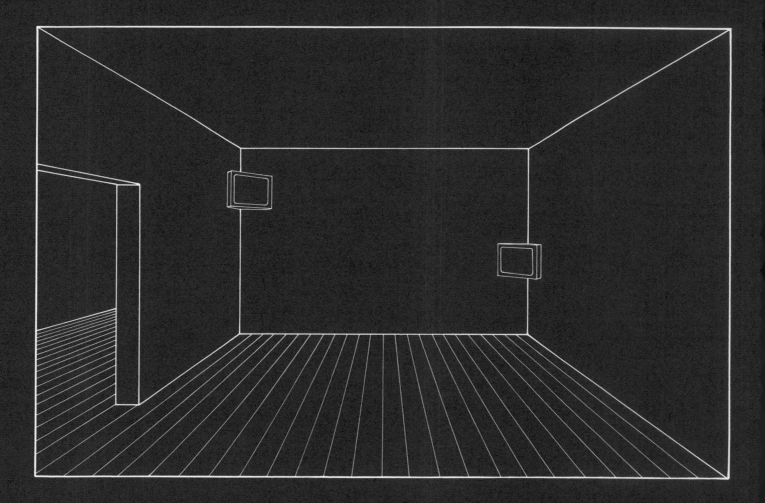

Towards a Post-Television Society

shop

After the Revolution

The post-television society: we can only just begin to feel it intuitively, but it already exists. We are currently seeing the first signs of a society in which the revolution inspired by television has come to an end: a society in which television may therefore be said to have completed its own 'destiny', to have finally come of age.

Paradox and Contrast

Television has turned the planet into a single, mighty organism, one which experiences history simultaneously in all its parts. A war, or a concert, wherever it takes place, is a stimulus perceived by this organism in real time. Information travels directly from the farthest edge of the globe right into our television set.

News and entertainment have become so entangled that they are now interchangeable. As it unfolds, all history is turned into entertainment, and dramas present a world just as real as the true one.

The television revolution is complete, having produced permanent modifications in our behaviour: in today's society, television is present but has become ornamental.

Our participation in events increases and at the same time decreases. Our awareness of tragedy going on around us grows, and with it our moral and political involvement; but simultaneously everything becomes more counterfeit, indirect – in the end, just another television docudrama.

The remote control allows us to change the channels of reality, to experience different true stories, different histories, different modes of behaviour. In this way, society has become polytheistic, syncretistic, and eclectic. At the same time it has also become substantially more monotheistic, precisely because of the standardised nature of the information that it receives.

Changed Behaviour

In the half-lit world which is the domain of the cathode-ray tube and which has become the new condition of our existence, the television revolution is now over. Our behaviour has been permanently modified by the medium. In this sense, what awaits us cannot be anything but a post-television society: a society in which the television is present, not as before, but as a system of decoration; a world in which the cathode-ray image ceases to be at the centre of the home but becomes more highly integrated, moving into many different corners of our environment. The screen presents an image that is seen but, except on special occasions, not looked at. It proffers information, circulating it like air being circulated by the air-conditioning system. It emits light, not intrusively, but as subdued as a Brian Eno concert; light which, like air conditioning, is absorbed through our skin, a surface of light consumption. In other words, the television screen is once again becoming an element of interior decoration, like a painted ornament or picture that is looked at occasionally but for the most part ignored.

Our capacity to absorb various sets of information at once has increased, and through a sort of remote control built into our perceptual system we are able to select in real time the media channel that interests us.

As Derrick de Kerckhove says, the power of communication is enormous. We are the ones that have changed. Our capacity to take in several types of information at once has increased enormously: television, radio, conversation, exchanges of glances, reading. These information systems form a sort of plankton all around us, a liquid and multimedia space which we inhabit. Using a sort of remote control built into our system of perception, we are able to select from among the many media and messages there present those that interest or concern us most, all in real time.

Television in the Home

In contrast to the views of many sociologists, I do not believe that television has ever modified the organisation of the home. It may have modified our behaviour, our culture, and even our physiology, but it has not changed the houses we live in.

It has become part of the domestic scene and yet has remained an awkward guest, a presence that is not provided for. It is asymmetrical with respect to the axes around which

The television has become an environmental system: it is no longer a point in space but a circuit, a spatial quality, an environmental 'microclimate'.

the traditional house is arranged. The television set, placed on a provisional table, has always remained at an angle, in a corner, movable, even if no one moves it. This means that the television set has never become the hearth or totem; it has remained *alongside* the hearth, a complement to other totems. Even though the television occupies our time, it does not occupy our space.

In practice, the telematic house has never existed and indeed will never exist. This is because the real nature of electronic technology and information does not lie in its capacity to organise actual space, but in its ability to create another, virtual, cathode-ray space. While electrical appliances have taken over the kitchen, the television set, like the telephone and the personal computer, has remained a temporary guest in the space of the home, space which is still organised on the basis of completely different anthropological laws.

All this is positive and quite new: information does not deform our physical space, but intervenes to create another and immaterial level of relations, a transverse network for the reception of information services.

In a short space of time we have learned to use the television as an environmental system, that is, as a visual presence within a multiple circuit of different kinds of information. We watch television while reading a book, listening to the radio, talking to other people, working, driving, walking. The television is not a point but a circuit, a spatial quality, a sort of informational microclimate to be consumed by the senses: a sort of new and diffuse environmental decoration.

Television Design

All these considerations greatly influence the way in which a television set is designed. Historically, the television set derives its form from the radio: first made of wood, then of Bakelite, and finally enclosed in a black case. From the television set as protagonist, we have moved to an anonymous television set, not intrusive in its form, but present as a service. The next step is that of its integration into the setting and into the furnishings.

Let me explain: the television set ceases to be an autonomous reality and becomes a system integrated into space – in the corners of the architecture, in the ceiling, inside other objects. The problem presented by the television set is not when it is switched on (because then it does not exist), but when it is switched off. It is the same for all the other household appliances, which have become a diffuse system: alive when they are working, and dead boxes cluttering up the home when they are turned off.

I therefore planned my workshop with the young designers of Philips along lines that are in keeping with my natural approach to the subject. In other words, I sought to focus the attention of our group not on questions of design or form, but on a set of problems, a system of reflections deriving from an analysis of reality; a system which can be used to derive innovative strategies for design, based on other factors than the information we obtain from marketing.

Being a Designer, Being a Consumer

The market has become the most obscure point in the whole industrial system. It is no longer possible today for any new theory of economics or management to be based on reliable information as far as the behaviour of consumers is concerned. Once they were a point of certainty for Franklin Taylor; today they are the point of uncertainty for everyone.

63

The only true guarantee in design is the cultural maturity of the designer, and the feeling that he is an integral and homogeneous part of society and the market.

If industry wants to produce new ranges of merchandise it has to rely on its capacities for design, that is, on its ability to propose, to be bold and creative. These are all activities which can be advanced by information and by analysis of the current situation, but which at the same time call for a risky synthesis, a logical leap towards the new.

My profession is that of designer, and designing today increasingly means inventing with courage, though not in a gratuitous manner. It has been said that when you design you are always on your own, in the sense that the decisions in the process of design can only be taken personally (or as a group), and there is never any total guarantee that they will be the right ones. The only true guarantee is provided by the cultural maturity of the designer, and by the feeling that he is an integral and homogeneous part of society and the market. The designer who lives outside this reality will always fail. Being a designer today does not mean being *different*, but being the *same* as others.

What the consumer wants is the same thing that we want, too: serious things, the right products, simple realities. But coming up with them is difficult, because simplicity is the fruit of the most highly evolved complexity. Otherwise it is merely the style of poverty.

 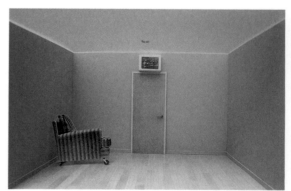

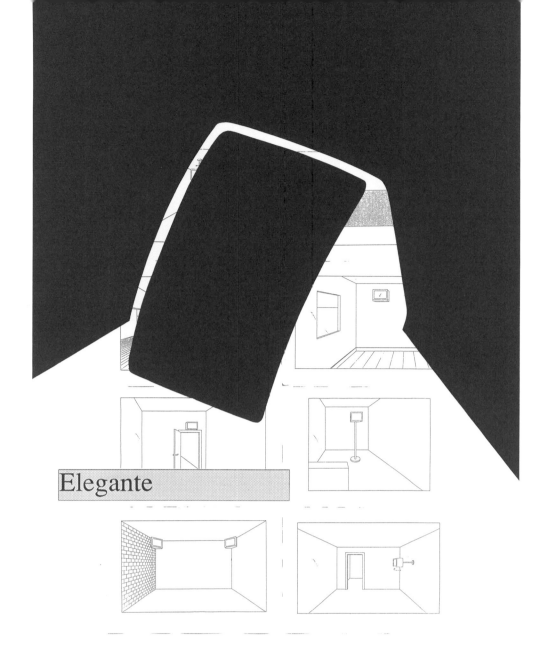

Elegante

In mapping the past, new media supplement the old. We can relive old battles, satisfy our curiosity. Meanwhile, the telelibrarian wags an electronic finger, gently reminding us of traditional library etiquette.

Help Desk

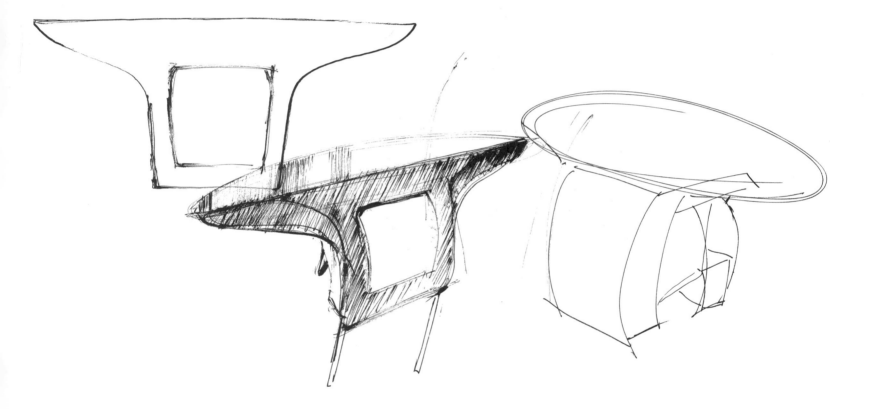

I considered television as a non-space-specific object. My table-top set contains an element of camouflage, but even so it can hardly be described as subliminal. The humble origins of its component parts are clearly visible.

Lacides Marquez

In another of my designs, I saw the
set as a monolith: omnipresent and
anonymous, not needing to be
integrated because always capable of
turning into something else – a table,
a pillow, a sculpture…

Lacides Marquez

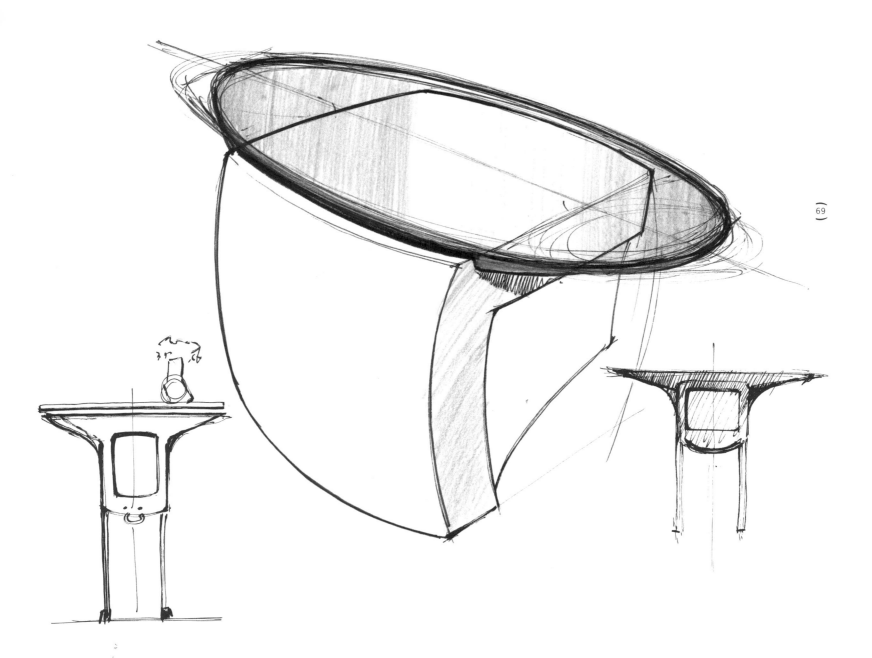

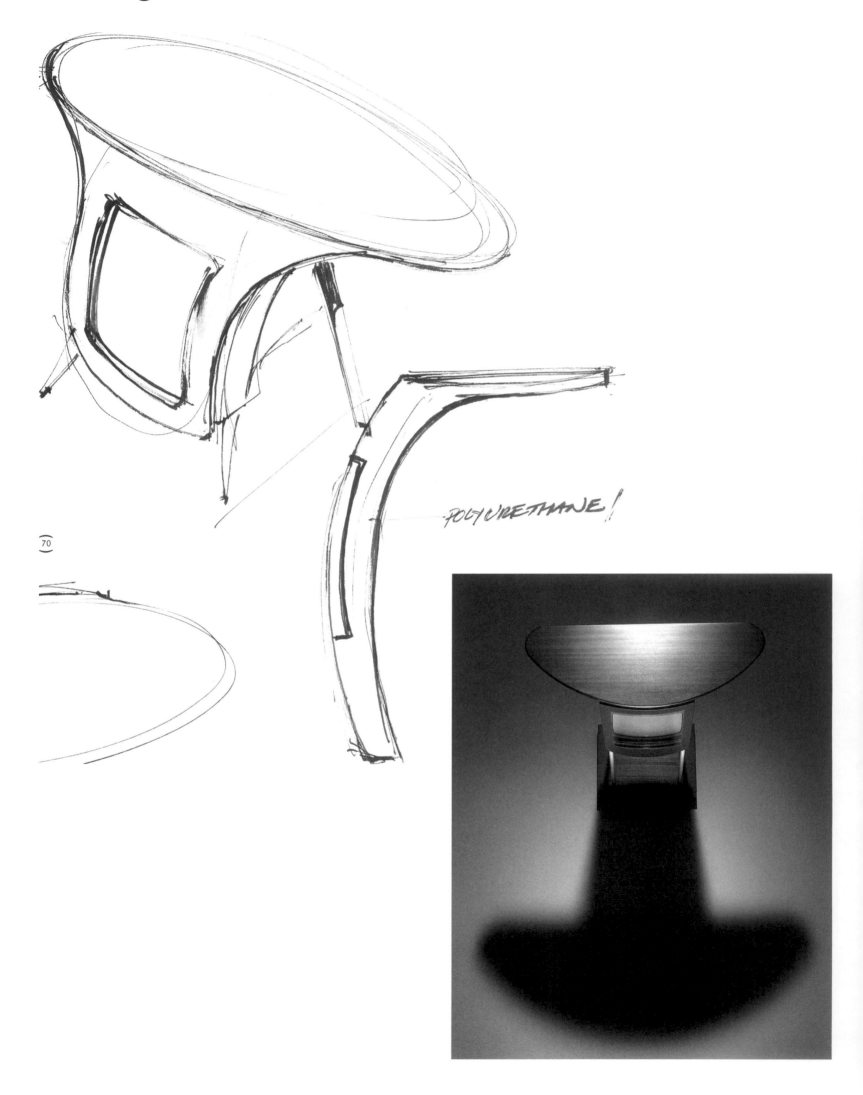

POLYURETHANE!

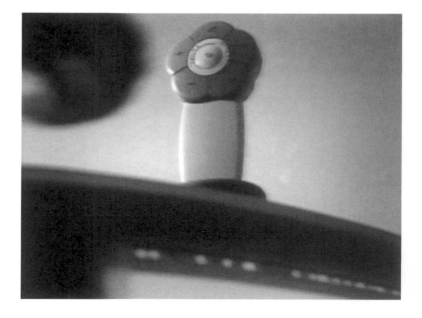

Growth

experience

TV climate-monitoring and expert advice help

create ideal conditions for plant growth. A flowery

remote ensures 'green control'. You'll be surprised

at the results...

Devoid of styling, the simple form of
this design is not based on aesthetic
considerations. Rather, it is the result
of a rationalisation of environmental
space and the technological givens of
tube and chassis.

Graham Hinde

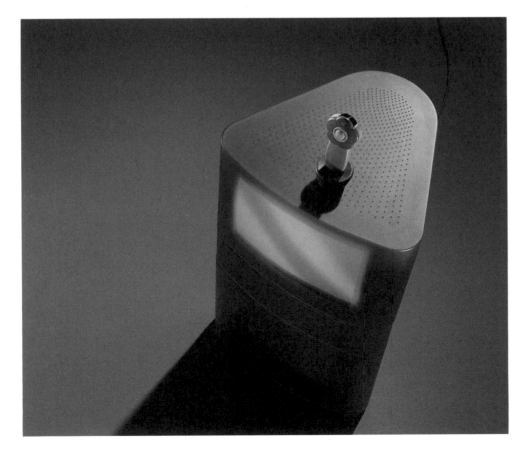

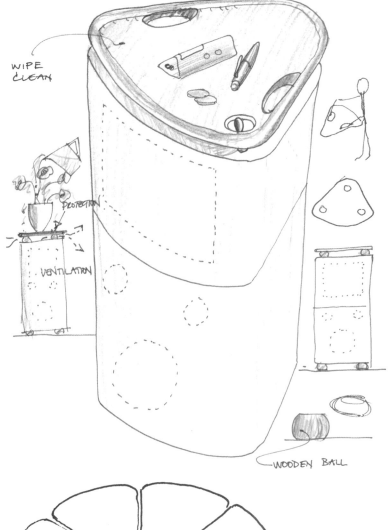

WIPE
CLEAN

PROTECTION

VENTILATION

WOODEN BALL

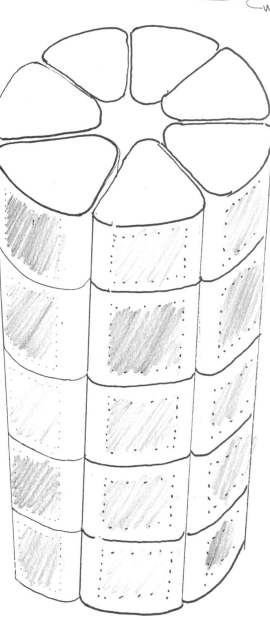

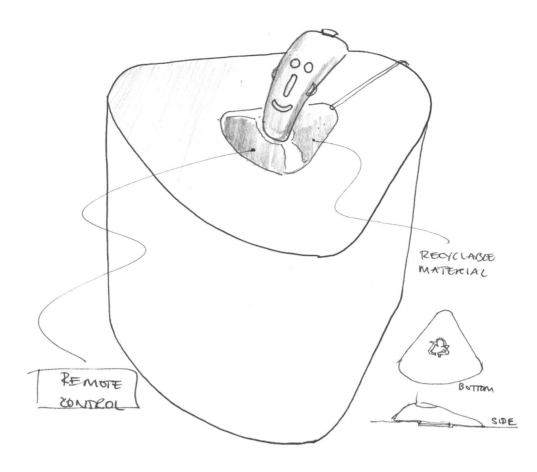

RECYCLABLE
MATERIAL

REMOTE
CONTROL

BOTTOM

SIDE

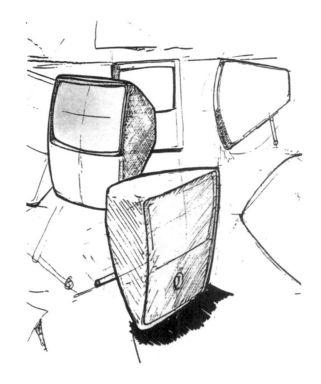

Vanishing trick

Unobtrusively lighting the room, this almost
invisible TV is always ready to tell us what we
need to know – the time, the weather, the best
place to be...

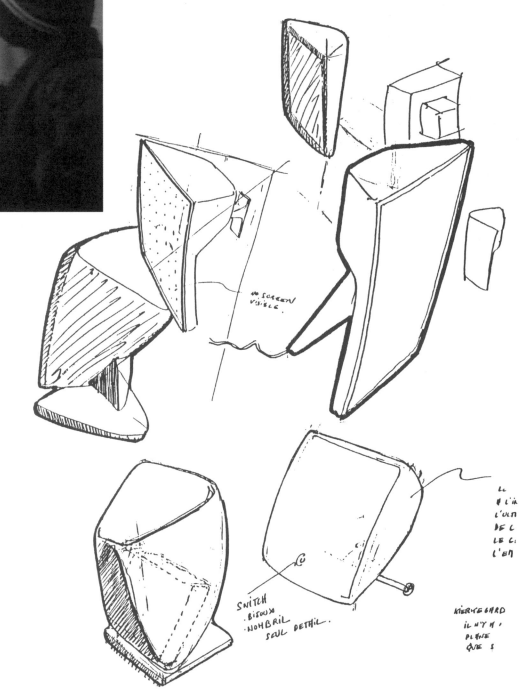

NO SCREEN VISIBLE.

SWITCH
BISOUX
NOMBRIL
SEUL DETAIL.

IL N'Y A
L'ULTI
DE L
LE C
L'EN

KIERKEGARD
IL N'Y A
PLENE
QUE S

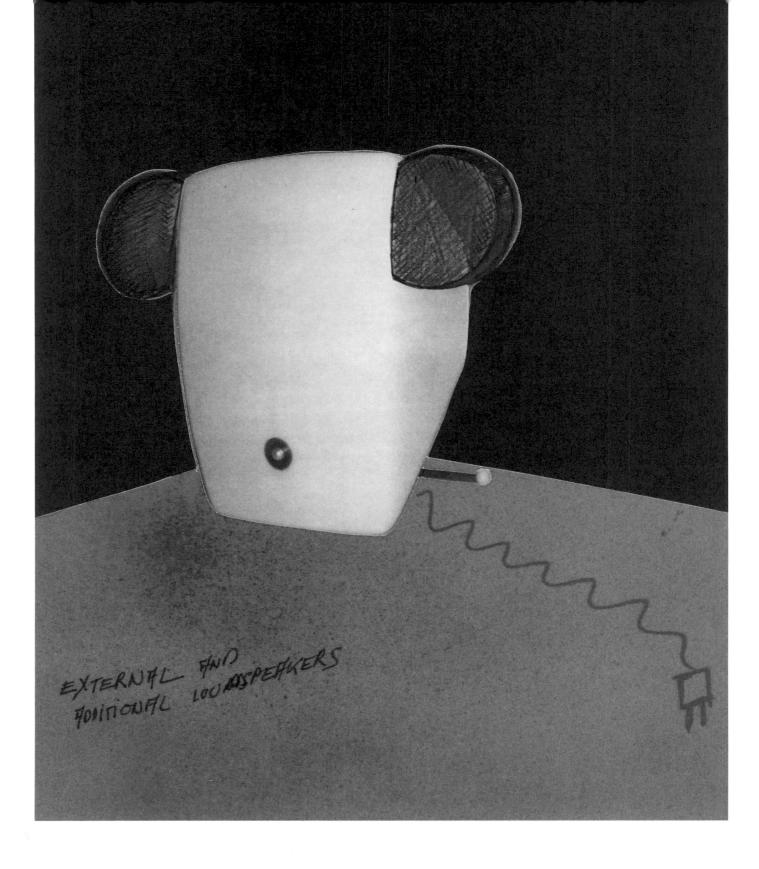

A white television

A humble, virgin object.
Whiter than white,
an in-depth white resulting from white layers.
The white of white stockings, of white bodies.
A white quality different from plastic white.
A white light. A quiet white, so different
from the aggressiveness of screen blue in the night.

Bertrand Richez

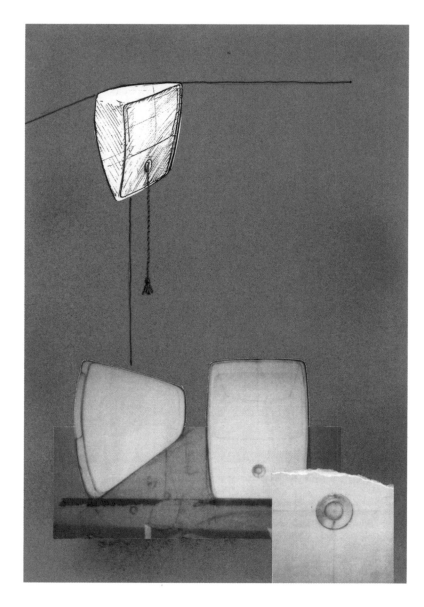

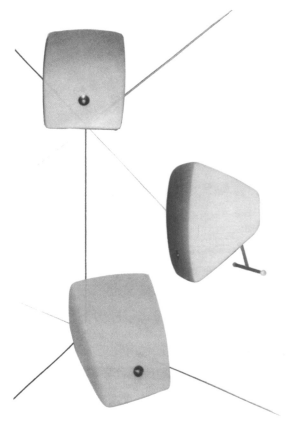

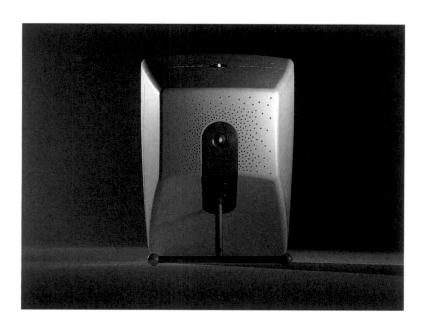

Refined, sophisticated

A milky skin, dressed only in a jewel,
a gold barbarian detail, a navel,
a cyclops' eye.
The only detail to stress its essence.
Called to serve by a tug on a bell-rope.
A tool, a familiar and daily invader.
Cuddling our children with its tyrannical presence.

Bertrand Richez

A special occasion deserves a special cake and a
special decor. What shall we choose?
A Renaissance palace? Everything's ready: now the
guest of honour. Call her on the videophone.
"Happy Birthday, darling!"

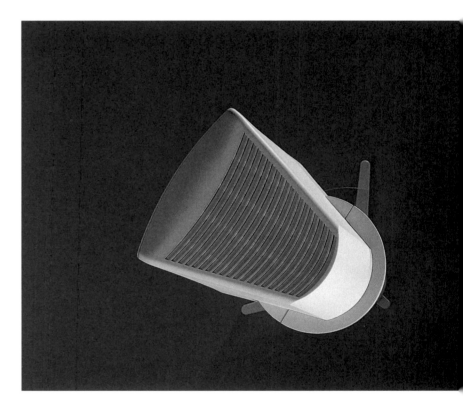

Celebration Scene

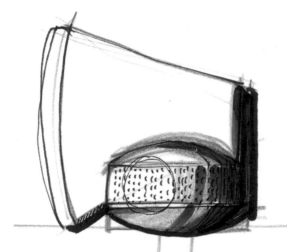

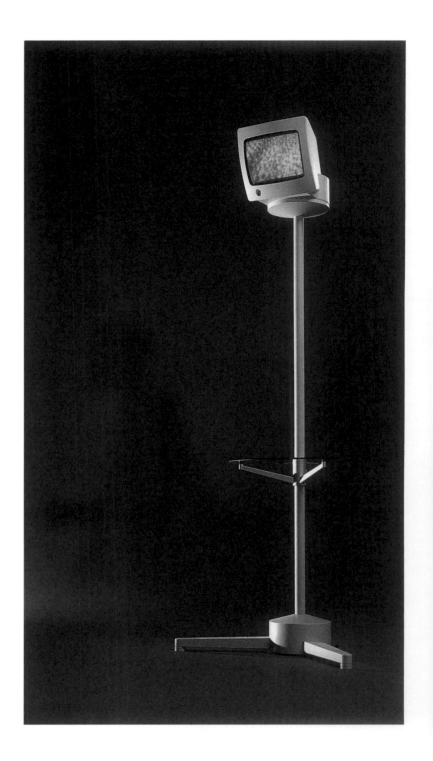

We gained insight into a different way
of working. Guided by a Master who
expressed strong views about the
concepts we produced, the easiest
response was to acquiesce. But it
soon became clear that this would
not work – we had to stand up for our
own ideas. More than ever before,
I became aware of the covert
restrictions we put on our work.

Paul Bas

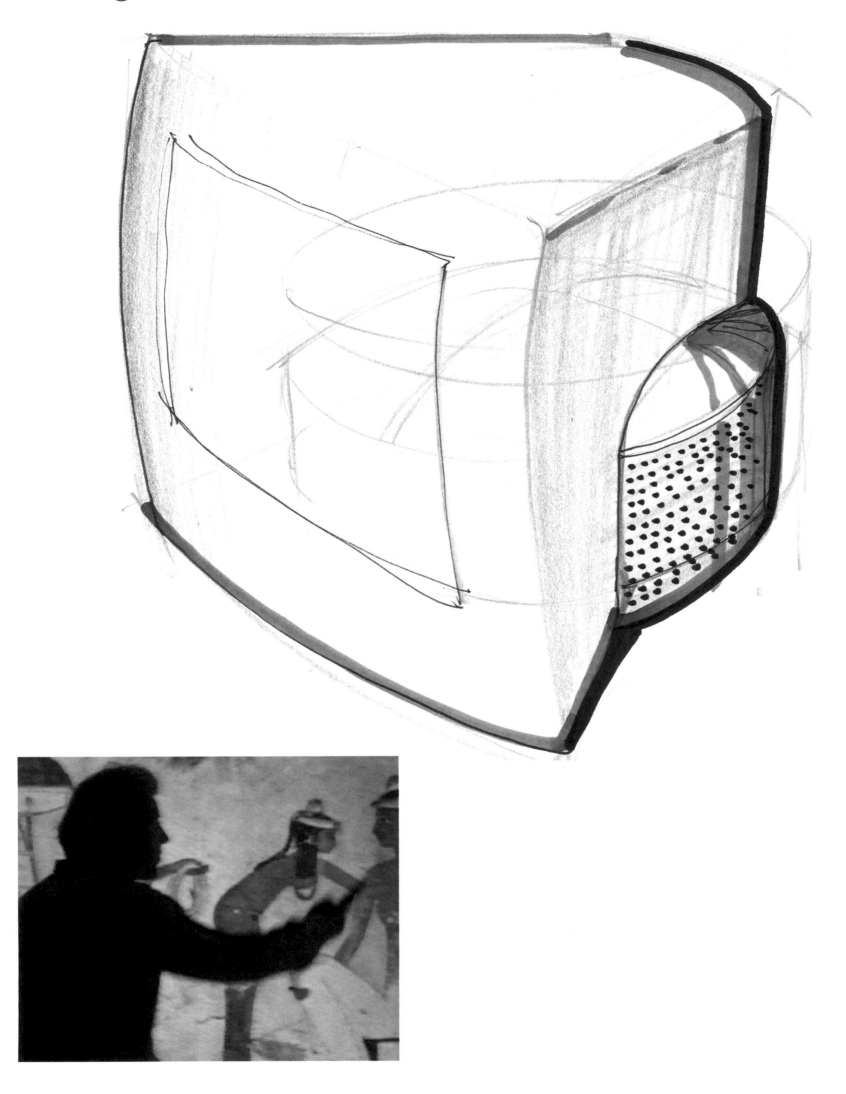

Roadside Romance:

TV Marries Computer

on the Electronic

Highway

Derrick de Kerckhove

The New Media Context

Even the slowest government bureaucracies are waking up and warming to the idea that the 'electronic superhighways' people talk about are just as critical to their survival, if not more so, than the upkeep of concrete roadways and parking lots. This realisation comes from various factors. The most obvious are economic: after all, television, the video side of the established market, has ruled the mind and marketable reality of most of the world since the early sixties. The rapid growth of personal computers since the early eighties has demonstrated that the screen could also be the focus of endless variations of domestic products and perhaps rival the motor industry for the support of national economies.

What are the key elements and the major new conditions of the electronic highways that should affect the future of television and of the economy?
– Digitisation, the discovery of 0/1, the smallest common denominator of everything that can be simulated, and, in effect, the new common sense;
– Networks, the development of live interactive fields for instant combining, testing and applying of new discoveries, new ideas, new techniques;
– Universal Access, which spells the reversal of an economy of scarcity into an economy of abundance.

Digitisation

0/1

It is important to acknowledge the Morse code as the 'missing link' between the alphabet and the computer. The translation of the 26 letters of the alphabet into three signs (long, short, zero) amounted to a radical refinement of the code, just as international wiring for telegraphic and, later, telephone communications established the first model of a 'common carrier' for networked intelligence. Of course, to achieve the universal flexibility of the binary code, a further reduction from three to two signs was critical. The binary digit is the smallest common denominator of everything that can be simulated: there is no need to cut up the binary digit any further. Today, digitisation has superseded both money and the alphabet as the main parsing device, becoming the new universal translator of all heterogeneous substances.

Convergence

While television and video technologies, following photography and cinema, were primarily concerned with the conquest of our mental space, computer networks emphasise the mastery of time inherent in the telegraphic and telephone systems. In terms of distributed intelligence, the role of television is to unify different fields of consciousness into large segments of spatialised cognition and to introduce a focused collective information-processing device in everyone's home. When TV began by adding the visual component to the existing radio network, though still a one-way medium, it was installing a kind of active collective memory in the culture. TV extends private cognition into the collective realm by reproducing on an external screen the main sensory combinations that we use to make sense internally. Especially when used for live broadcasting, TV supplies a common referent supplemented by three key sensory inputs: hearing, sight and kinaesthetic proprioception. Within a relatively short time in its technical development, TV has managed to manifest its latent tendency to bring the spectator into the scene of the action. Today's TV accomplishes this by offering an increasing number of interactive options from humble zapping to video recording, editing and video-conferencing. Such developments herald the democratisation of the medium. The trend from broadcasting to narrowcasting and direct input from the viewer is still being worked on in technologies such as set-top boxes and 'telecomputers'.

Telecomputer

It is instructive to understand the development of computers not in opposition to but in continuity with TV. In the new buzzword, *telecomputer*, you will notice that both the idea of 'vision' and even that of 'television' have disappeared. The key element of *telecomputer* is *tele,* that is, the distant connecting device (for example, the telephone). What emerges from the terminology is the notion of telecom combined with computer. This is because, very soon, in our digital, full service, networked information environments, all of the realm of television will actually be swallowed up by computers. Take High Definition TV (HDTV), for example, an innovation which has much less to do with definition than with digitisation. HDTV is television graduating to the status of computers. Indeed, computers now linked by telephones inherit TV's most precious legacy, namely its access to large numbers of people at once in real time. However, with telecomputers, people can actually talk to each other, they can get in on the act. Whatever was dumb about TV becomes extremely intelligent on the telecomputer.

Not so evident is the combined psychological appeal of the technologies themselves: while television has always been perceived as a broadcast medium, with a largely public character, computers were soon personalised as stand-alone, private media. While TV provided a kind of collective mind for everyone, but with no individual input, computers were private minds without collective inputs. Convergence offers a new, unprecedented possibility, that of plugging individuals and their special needs into collective minds. This new situation is profoundly empowering; it has social and political as well as economical repercussions. It will accelerate changes and adaptations in the geopolitical scene as well as in the private sensibility of us all. It will bring on new forms of consciousness and put new pressures on the world's educational systems to cope with the change. It will also take most markets by surprise. Indeed, while it is obvious that, short of a major political or social catastrophe, the globalisation of the world will take that route, it is not quite so clear what we are going to do with all this communication power. How do you change the habit of relying on the motorcar for power, action and prestige into the adoption of 'telepresence' as a way of being?

Networks

The recent tendency of computers to become networked is another key to the new feeling, the incipient psychology of the developing convergence. Suddenly, the telephone networks and the telecommunication companies, which were powerful and effective but usually ignored by public and private sector concerns, are coming to the front of our collective consciousness. Cable companies in countries such as the US and Canada are vying with the telephone companies to offer multimedia services, video-conferencing and video-on-demand by compressed and digitised signals. Nets, internets and ethernets are growing in rapid spurts like the brain of a world-size developing child. Since the telecomputer is not quite there yet, let us examine the Internet as an intermediate technology.

The Internet, today's best example of an 'Electronic Highway'

The Internet is a network of networks which allows very precise narrowcasting and puts the control in the hands of the user. The Net is not invasive, because, unlike the telephone, it doesn't call you, you call it. A single message of distress on the Net can very quickly trigger one or more pertinent responses. In the electronic sea, the message in the bottle is sure to get there on time. The nice thing about the Net is that you can tap it through cellular technology, too. Digitised data doesn't have to come down a pipe. With 20 million users in over 90 countries, the Net is growing at the rate of doubling every ten months. It is also capable, when connected directly to fibre or main trunks, to provide hypermedia interactivity, with networked multimedia coming fast upon its heels. Users pay for what they ask for, and can get directly to the source without having to clear fee-levying gateway keepers.

The Net is a monumental computer all by itself, with astounding organic memory banks and parallel processors numbering today over 20 million, tomorrow a billion coprocessors. Why call that a highway? The Internet is really a brain, a collective, living brain clicking as you read. It is a brain (like yours and mine) that never ceases to work to think, to produce information, to sort it, to combine it, etc. Of course, it is still in its infancy and pretty messy. The main issue of the Net is how to plug into it and how to navigate in it. That is still a problem for many would-be users. We go at it with our TV-generation minds, looking for colour and movement and instant gratification, and we find grey, dry, bookish and slow data. But the times are still changing. The Internet is 'going hyper' and is about to provide those who can connect to it directly on main trunk lines with the first real on-line multimedia with the World Wide Web full-colour, fully interactive services. In more ways than one, the Internet has all the super-duper highway hype beat by a large measure. It comes from below, from the underground, the subconscious level of our collective intelligence. And, just like that subconscious level, it is made up of much too much data for all of it to be filtered at the conscious level. This is why larger units of processing and distribution are necessary.

Bandwidth

What is happening? Just as they eventually became wired for the telephone, private homes as well as public offices are about to be wired for full data and video bandwidth. There are presently many different standards and capacities which include many different telecom networks such as ISDN (Integrated Services Digital Networks) and, in some countries, cabling which can carry up to 900 million bits per second, but is not yet switched for digitisation nor wired for interactive response. Governments and local industries are considering the options of incrementally going from standard analog lines, which will be digitised so that they can carry about 64,000 bits per second, to what the industry calls T3 lines, with a capacity of 45 million bits per second. This capacity would allow fully interactive transmission of data, sound, images and video. However, even as decisions are being taken in ministries and industry, breakthroughs in technology – such as asymmetrical digital subscriber loop (ADSL), which allows sending of full-motion video on standard telephone lines – are changing the rules of the game.

The question is further complicated by the fact that wires and airwaves are no longer alone in vying to provide us with a conduit to collective mental processes. Cable networks are now generating their own brands of markets. Wired networks are different from airwaves because their image, and consequently their effect, is much closer to that of the human nervous system, but then extended from the individual body to the social body. Broadcasting in the airwaves, however, creates a soft, light and vibratory environment which resembles our mind. And with the rapidly growing cellular technologies, yet another kind of relationship between individuals and public space is developing.

When they are not battling each other or obsolete government regulations, these three simultaneous universes of communication are more or less self-organising, as they discover and refine their own character and how best they should be used. MIT guru and Media Lab Director Nicholas Negroponte says that TV and radio should move out of the airwaves altogether and leave the airspace for cellular communications, which are the more urgent ones.[1] He may be right: there is nothing worse than a foggy brain when there is an emergency. TV and radio are part of the white noise which is needed for an organism to survive, but they don't have to monopolise the front stage of our collective consciousness all the time.

Radical decentralisation

With the number of different initiatives in technical, industrial, legal and political realms, it is not easy to predict where all this activity is leading and what a stabilised technological environment will look like. Ideally, the airwaves should be like the air itself, that is, really free for people to act in real time, not in some preprogrammed reality. Broadcasting is fairly invasive and only the people who use it should pay for it. With video-on-demand looming rapidly on the horizon, the public communications scene is turning private, looking more like telecommunications and less like broadcasting. George Gilder predicts the rapid demise of broadcasting in a world of electronic highways and the rise of widely available and inexpensive communications which will turn the whole relationship around: "Television and telephone systems – designed for a world in which spectrum or bandwidth was scarce – are utterly unsuited for a world in which bandwidth is abundant. The key strategy of both systems has been to centralise intelligence in local central offices, cellular base stations, cable television nodes, and broadcast centres, and give the user a stripped-down commodity terminal, whether a telephone or television set". Gilder adds that "Over the next decade, engineers will use bandwidth and computer power on the edges of networks as a substitute for switching and intelligence at the centre...First to fall will be the broadcast system of a few thousand stations and a few networks serving millions of idiot boxes."[2]

Pay-per-bit

The ideal condition will be that people will be able to choose – and pay for – as much bandwidth and as many bits as they need at any time in the course of their communications. This is called 'pay-per-bit' or 'bandwidth-on-demand' marketing, which appeals to more enlightened critics as the most democratic and most economically efficient way of wiring the country. Viewers and listeners will buy the time and the items they need in a 'pay-per-bit' addressable database network of networks. They will also pay per bit and per point for any casting they care to do.

Market Implications of Universal Access

If information is truly the staple of today's economy, we should keep in mind that, unlike our natural resources, information is the only substance that actually grows rather than

1 'Trading places: Over the next 20 years, television and telecommunications will swap their primary means of transmission', in 'Products and services for computer networks', *Scientific American*, Sept. 1991, pp. 76-78.

2 'The end of telephony', 150 Economist Years, special anniversary issue of *The Economist*, 1993, p. 76.

depletes with use. We are looking at an economy of abundance. This development, of course, will only occur when the infrastructure allows universal access. Universal access will come by nature or by force, though it may take a political and social revolution. Just as the old monarchic power structures had to be toppled to make room for the body of the people in the democratic process, the present establishment of communications and information control may have to be zapped out of existence. The transition has already begun quite peacefully, thanks to the increased sophistication of domestic production technologies. The shift of controls from the producer/broadcaster to the consumer/user will turn a sizeable minority of users into their own producers, or, as Alvin Toffler calls the new figures in the workplace, 'prosumers'.

The decentralising of broadcasting will be accompanied by the decentralising of production technology. As prices of video and computer equipment go down, quality and performance go up. Today it is possible to achieve better results with a semi-professional camcorder, a computer-assisted desktop video editor and a simple sound mixing table, than used to be attainable with huge editing rooms and long time-delays. Transmitter technology, spurred by cellular networks, will also put casting power in the hands of individuals over larger and larger areas.

From 'couch potatoes' to 'couch guerillas'

The deeper reason why the market will support such developments in spite of the threats they pose to established broadcasters is that the multiplication of channels via satellite, cable, telephone compression and cellular transmission will require more and more content, implying that ordinary people, even 'couch potatoes', will have to contribute to this content themselves. People will develop their own regular network, for business or for pleasure, without restrictions of time or place. Video-on-demand (VOD) is today's biggest future market commodity because people understand what it means; however, by the time VOD is in place, the bigger business item will be networked multimedia. As soon as the problems of copyright for multimedia content are resolved, interactivity will turn many info-consumers into info-providers and create a flurry of special interest markets and transnational communities which participate in them.

Videoconferencing

As quality videoconferencing with large and comfortable screens comes down in price, some people will still connect to standard analogue lines (perhaps with a special card added to convertible TV sets), but most will take advantage of improved compression ratios, capitalising on competitive advances and lower prices for digitally-switched twisted-pair copper wires and even fibre networks. At first, videoconferencing will remain more popular in business, government and academe than in the private home, where many people will resent it as an invasion of privacy and not see its advantage for cutting down on commuting. Later, videoconferencing will both create an enormous live and safe video sex market and simplify door-to-door salesmanship. Subsequently, portable cellular video-conferencing will accelerate the real-estate market, allowing people to visit anywhere from their residence. Videoconferencing will multiply conditions and opportunities for public surveys, unobtrusive polling, and, alas, also for fraud and for police surveillance. Overall, its most important effect will be to change home/workplace relationships more radically than the motorcar did in the average North American city. People will spend long periods of time far away from their place of business, preferably in the comfort and peace of their secondary residence, their country home. People who commute will go back to trains because they will favour the freedom of movement it gives them to control an intelligent machine, say a hand-held computer or a cellular telephone, over the obligation to control a dumb machine, a motorcar. Architecture and development will begin to plan and design in terms of the communications accessibility rather than in terms of the roadway and hydro infrastructures.

Interactive advertising

Advertising was really given a tremendous boost by mass media, and it supported economies of scale during the heyday of broadcast television. It is bound, at first, to suffer from the decentralisation at hand. Nobody knows quite how to make public use of computer networks financially profitable in any way other than by charging for the lines and for the time used. However, interactive multimedia, even the rather limited kind of interactivity allowed today on some cable-borne TV, show the direction of things to come. People actually like advertising and many stay up late at night in front of their TV sets just to watch 'infomercials'. They will like it even more if they can get 'into' their ad by selecting the process and the kind of information they are presented with. Furthermore, they will have a chance to respond directly to the supplier. Instead of a 'mass' market of one-way communications looking for large demographics, there will be a 'speed' market with two-way interactive feedforward and feedback.

Another major development is the developing possibility of finding out and recording the exact numbers of users and buyers for any product. All digital technologies converge to numbers with the greatest exactitude. There was a time in the market when you could fool most of the people most of the time. Today, an advertiser or a corporation cannot make any false claim about the real audience or the contents of the package: in electronic conditions, you cannot fool anybody anytime. In terms of how the human nervous system works, it makes much more sense to privilege communications which allow instant feedback on connections rather than spray-gunning reality with pellets of news, ads and services.

Intelligence in an Economy of Abundance

The sudden acceleration and multiplication of data produces chaos. Hence our newfound interest for chaos theory, dissipative structure theory and other weird thinking such as catastrophe theory. We would very much like to see all these huge developments organise themselves without too much interference on our part; and that may very well happen, though not necessarily without some loss. We have been trained so long to focus on scarcity that we don't quite know how to deal with abundance. This is a situation that calls for new kinds of intelligence.

We are in desperate need of filters

If the previous economy of the printed and mass media was based on production, the new economy of interactive media will be based on reduction, following the image of the brain, which some neurobiologists say is not a producing mechanism, but a sort of huge reducing valve to allow ordered operations to take place in the body. Says Toronto computer artist-engineer David Rokeby, remarking upon the bewildering opportunities

3. In an unpublished paper made available to me by the author.

presented by the flexibility of computer programming: "We are in desperate need of filters."[3] The jobs of the future will go to gatekeepers, intelligent assistants, information-hounds trained on the latest info about this or that. The big engineering contracts will go to encryption software for privacy and to the development of Personal Digital Assistant packages and devices to bring up instantly what you need at voice command. New forms of collective intelligence will develop, based on constantly self-updating statistical samplings, such as those that can already be obtained on the Internet about the concerns and activities of the various interest groups. They will be tuned to individual needs by keyword, inverted index searches and neurally networked integrators.

The value of ignorance

When everything is known somewhere by someone and is accessible for a price, you develop a 'just-in-time' kind of psychology. Why bother learning all this stuff yourself if you have access to it when you need it? Quite the reverse: you might find value in *not* knowing something, since the very process of discovering something may be more useful and exciting than the actual content of the discovery. When you have real expert systems, improved by sophisticated neural networks and with rapid learning curves, you don't need to be an expert in anything. Your best resource might well become your own ignorance, forcing your attention to reposition itself to learn what you need from the unique angle of the non-expert. We might all develop a taste and pride for the exact recognition and avowal of our limits and limitations. Our whole value system is now in the process of changing from hierarchical, competitive, aggression-based criteria of excellence to supportive-collaborative-interactive ones. In that new context, what will be needed more than ever is good judgment – and that comes from experience, not learning. Judgement is like intuition: part meaning, part feeling, arising from the collaboration of mind and body in synergy.

Interactivity is touch

Interactivity is a form of touch. All interactive systems present some form of tactile relationship between the human body and the environment. As Virtual Reality developer Jaron Lanier explains: "I think one of the striking things about a virtual world system in which you have the pliancy, the ability to change the content of the world easily, is that the distinction between your own body and the rest of the world is slippery. Essentially, from a virtual reality perspective, the definition of the body is that part which you can move as fast as you think. In a virtual world (...), you might be opening doors at a distance or exploding volcanoes on the horizon, or whatever it might be. At that point, it becomes difficult to really define what the boundary of the body is."[4] Indeed, just as the rapid elaboration of the point-of-view became the condition for individual freedom in the neutral space of renascent perspectivism, a proprioceptive appreciation of one's point-of-being in the instantly networked data-flow is among the conditions for retaining a measure of physiological and psychological control over one's whereabouts in electronic nomadism.

4. (with F. Biocca), 'An insider's view of the future of virtual reality', *Journal of Communication*, 42(4), 1992, p. 162.

The bottom line: the poor man's credit line

However, to business-minded people, all the above may just sound sentimental. A touch-sensitive intelligence may be good enough to win an argument with one's mate, but it doesn't affect the bottom line. However, that is precisely the question. In a world of plenty, how long will we find it useful to reduce everything to a single numerical evaluation and call it satisfying? Money, as it is still operant today, is simply not fast nor complex enough to act as a proper evaluation mechanism. Indeed, as it migrates to digital convergence in ATMs and EFTs, money is itself changing its nature. When money reaches the speed of light it becomes pure energy. It may not need to go through a symbolic stage at all. If we follow the trend of encryption technology, we can see that it will soon be easier to attach a quantitative measurement to all operations on the global common carrier, than to manage and store a material representation of value. The job of money will be confined precisely to the function of parsing the myriad digitised operations of our single global computer. In the economy of abundance, we will inevitably go to the 'pay-per-bit' and the 'definition-on-demand' formulas, with instant debit at the source, at the time of use, simply because currency and current will become the same thing.

In the computer, language meets light, one tapping the other directly: absolute energy meets absolute complexity. Lasers, fibre optics and electro-magnetic fields are the new building blocks of intelligence. Top speed will join top integration in quickly uniforming standards. That is the stuff of reality itself. The big reversal of our civilisation is occurring right now, and that is the reversal of conscious and unconscious realms. Not long ago, the world was dumb and we were clever. But the computer-assisted world is becoming very clever, and faster than we are. Very soon the collective technological intelligence will outperform the individual organic ones both in speed and integration. It will be interesting to see how this unified cognitive organisation will take care of the environment, of poverty, and what criteria it will dictate for genetic engineering. But for the time being, relax. We are not there yet.

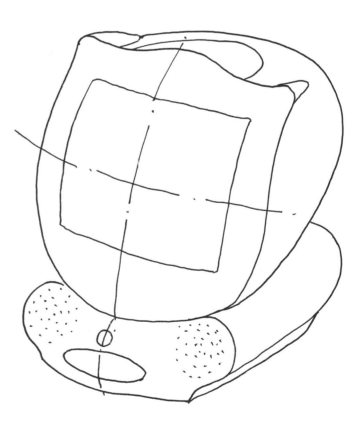

Stefano Marzano

w o r k

Into the Era of

Soul

s   h   o   p

The Metaphysics of Television

What is the nature of television? What are its first principles? I do not mean here its technology but rather its ultimate *esse*, and its deeper significance in our lives. Although no easy task, we certainly need to explore such questions if we are to design televisions appropriate for the twenty-first century. The way we interact with television is becoming increasingly complex and the need to improve our understanding of the medium is therefore all the more urgent.

All artefacts, I suggest, may be viewed as having two essential elements. I shall call them, by analogy with traditional metaphysics, the Body and the Soul. The Body comprises those characteristics of the artefact which give rise to nothing beyond themselves. They are limited, bound in time and space. They gain access to the human faculty of reason, but cannot penetrate the human imagination. The Soul, by contrast, comprises those aspects which are intangible and unlimited. By appealing directly to the human imagination, they trigger an infinity of ideas and emotions. Transcending the physical, they speak to the soul of the beholder.

In these terms then, a traditional object, such as a statue or a chair, can be said to have a Body (its physical form) and a Soul (the meaning, the associations and emotions, aesthetic or affective, aroused in the viewer or user). Television, however, in common with other products of high technology, has a more complex metaphysical structure, corresponding to its complex physical structure. At first sight, we might say that the Body of television is its hardware, i.e., the electronic circuitry, the screen, the controls, and the casing required for the device to operate effectively. Its Soul would then be its 'software', the programmes, the sounds and images which entertain, inform and inspire the viewers. Each, thus defined, is clearly a typical example of its category.

But such a structuring is too simplistic. The situation is complicated by the fact that a television has two modes of existence. It can be switched on or switched off.

When the television is on, our attention is directed exclusively towards the software, which, as we have said, can be seen as its Soul. Just as in a theatre, when the lights go down, all eyes are concentrated on the 'stage': the software is performing. We can be inspired by the stories it tells, we can be thrilled by the sensory input it offers us. But we can also identify a Body of this software: the form of the graphics, the style of the photography, the quality of the acting, and so on.

When the television is switched off, it is the hardware, the Body, that comes into its own. In its way, it too performs and displays its own Soul. The appearance of the set itself has meaning, communicating certain cultural and aesthetic values which have the power to inspire and delight.

With the tremendous expansion of possibilities provided by telecommunications, satellite broadcasting and multi-media, which expand the realm of the software, it is all too easy to push hardware, the carrier of the software, out of the limelight. But, of course, the hardware is necessary for television to exist at all. The software cannot achieve its end – the inspiration of the viewer – without the cooperation of the hardware. Similarly, the Body, without its immanent Soul, the software, loses its primary reason for existence. There is, in other words, a relation of interdependency between the two.

The Polycentric Home

A second issue that needs to be addressed is the way television relates to and functions in the domestic space, the home.

For several millennia, the development of domestic architecture has followed essentially the same pattern. It has been characterised by the progressive implementation of the concept of having separate areas devoted to separate tasks or functionalities. From an original single, open-plan living space, in which all activities took place, including the care and housing of domestic animals, the home has become increasingly subdivided by walls into monofunctional areas. The kitchen for cooking, the bedroom for sleeping, the dining room for dining, the bathroom for ablutions, and so on. In the same way, the fire, formerly a source of heat for cooking, of warmth for comfort, and consequently also the location of social activity, has now been dispersed around the house: fire for cooking to the kitchen, fire as social focus to the living room and fire as source of warmth throughout the house by means of central heating.

Although our domestic architecture still adheres to the traditional concept of monofunctional areas, there is now overlaying it a new, virtual matrix. This new matrix is a remapping of living 'space' based on leisure and social activities, rather than on functions. The home has become polycentric; rooms have become multifunctional. One member of the family may be playing with the computer in the bedroom, another may be watching television in the study, a third may be reading in the living room and a fourth telephoning in the kitchen. They may eat formally in the dining room or informally in the kitchen, in the sitting-room on a tray, or have breakfast in bed. We can prepare food in the kitchen, cook fondue in the sitting room, or barbecue in the garden.

This development is a reflection of the increasing fragmentation and individualisation of industrial and post-industrial societies. People today are more individualistic, no longer following clearly pre-defined patterns of behaviour. No more do children automatically follow in their parents' footsteps. Families are becoming communities of individuals, just as consumers in general are moving away from group style towards individual style. They are making their own choices, creating their own 'culturosphere', rather than simply adopting the values of others.

Both this process of individualisation and the evolution of the home into a polycentric environment have affected the role of television in the domestic setting. Initially, as a newcomer, television was assigned a peripheral position in the home, the corner of the sitting room. Despite this lowly status, it quickly became the new point of focus for domestic life, the source of entertainment and information. Psychologically at least, it moved to centre-stage. In this respect, it usurped the role of the hearth, around which tales were once told and exploits recounted. The television took over the parts of story-teller and minstrel alike, and provided the flickering light and psychological warmth that made us feel truly at home.

But just like the fire, physically, the television is now being dispersed throughout the house – to the bedroom, the kitchen, the study and maybe even the bathroom. We can watch the channel we like, at the time we like, in the environment we like. The participation of television in the restructuring of the home from a monocentric to a polycentric environment means that television is on the eve of a radical transformation. It will develop beyond its present virtual monomorphism to become truly polymorphic. It will cease to be monofunctional and will take on new roles. In short, it will start to do and be exactly what we want.

Domesticated Technology

Technology was once an alien in our familial scene. The television was initially housed in a wooden box and placed uneasily in a corner. Now, however, such technology is rapidly becoming domesticated. We now feel that many of the technological products that share our homes are as dear – or at least as significant – to us as pets or friends. There are many more such 'friends' just waiting to be invited in to join us, and television is likely to be the focus for many of them.

The new personalised settings in the polycentric home will give rise to new forms of the set itself. Until recently, sets varied little in their general characteristics. With few exceptions, they were not designed to fit precisely into the setting in which they would appear. But as the number of televisions per household increases, there will be a greater need for different-looking models. The decorative quality of the hardware will come to play an increasingly important role, expressing its own personalised visual character.

In the bedroom, for example, we will curl up intimately with our mini-screen TV, children will watch it secretly under the bedclothes or talk to it like a teddy-bear. In another room, we shall create our own wide-screen cinema – basking in an all-enveloping sensory experience, enjoying the sense of *being there*. And in another area of the home, the television may also, as I hinted at above, fulfil the role of *objet d'art*. It may inspire and please us aesthetically simply by virtue of its outward appearance – what I referred to above as the Body of the hardware.

In short, we shall all want our own set to express our own personality and satisfy our own individual needs. But the needs that can be met will go far beyond those that television technology is currently able to address. Technologies are converging fast. Already television, telecommunications and computer technologies are being integrated.

Others will undoubtedly follow. This development will lead to a whole new range of functions and a whole new range of needs that they can satisfy.

Interactivity

One of the most significant consequences of the fusion of various digital technologies will be interactive television. The effect of television over the past few decades on social intercourse has been dramatic. But it is an effect that has been something of a two-edged sword.

On the local level, television initially resulted in a degradation of social interaction. When people started staying at home to watch television instead of going out to the theatre, the cinema or the sports stadium, the group experience became an individual experience. Once we used to be in the physical presence of performers and players, though we related to them only from our status as members of a crowd. Now, on television, often alone, we view only a two-dimensional image but can none the less enter into a quasi-intimate relationship with the people on the screen. At the same time, the family changed from being a genuine group, engaging in mutually stimulating activities, to a group of individuals, physically present together, but, as they watch television, each individually involved in a virtually exclusive relationship with the screen. Locally, then, television has led to a deterioration in the quality of social intercourse. The relation between the members of the family or social group has changed. Stimuli are now sought outside the family circle, and not on a group basis but alone.

On the global level, however, television has expanded our horizons enormously. Combining as it does the two fundamental senses of sound and vision, it allows us to perceive and experience – in more realistic ways than ever before – parts of the world we are perhaps incapable of reaching physically. Our social awareness on the macro level has been raised to heights previously unknown. The vast array of images to which we now have access also gives us similarly increased access to the immaterial world, inspiring fantasies and engendering dreams.

Thus television seems to have diminished two-way communication on the local level, while enhancing one-way communication on the global level. But we are now about to enter the era of interactive television. As we move from passive watching to interactive televiewing, we shall at least be moving towards integral social communication at global level, a development which may go some way towards restoring the balance between social and individual activity, between communication at the local and at the global level.

Certainly, one of the social benefits that television has provided has been that many people have been able to experience human contact which they would otherwise have been denied. The elderly and housebound have been able to remain informed about the outside world; the lonely have felt they have had company. But so far this contact has only been passive; people have been placed in the role of voyeurs, powerless to exert any influence on what they observe. Now, with the coming of interactive television, they will be able to participate in more genuine social interaction through this medium. In addition, with the increasing individualisation of telecommunications and television transmission, people will be able to communicate interactively with loved ones living far away. Young people will be able to be present at happenings of their choice all over the world. Those who for one reason or another are unable to travel will be able to enter and experience other cultures.

Expanding Experience

However, interactive television, though arguably the most significant consequence of converging technologies to emerge so far, is not the only one. Let us just speculate for a moment on a few more intriguing possibilities.

We all cherish moments and experiences shared with loved ones. School friends, first loves, happy holidays, children's smiles, and parents or grandparents no longer with us. What is now represented by photograph albums, home videos, or that bundle of love-letters tied up with ribbon could soon be integrated into a digital 'home treasure-house', an ever-accessible visual and aural record of our history, an aide-mémoire to help us get more from our memories and the special collective experience which is family and friendship.

Television is in a sense an extension of our eyes, but we have no control over where the camera is directed. But suppose we add an extra 'eye' to our television, a small movable camera? Those with failing eyesight could use it to magnify writing or printing, with the enlarged text being displayed on the television screen. Elderly people or the house-bound used to sit by the window, watching the world go by. But that's not always easy in a modern high-rise building – unless you have an electrical eye on a flexible neck. They could use it to keep in touch with life just outside their home through the television screen. A camera linked to the television would do away with the need for mirrors, with their built-in disadvantage of lateral image reversal. And we could even wash, shave or make up, looking at ourselves in the bathroom 'TV mirror', while in a corner of the same screen we watch the latest news and weather on breakfast television.

In the traditional home, the fire not only provided warmth, but it also served as an object of meditation, stilling the mind and freeing the spirit. Gazing into a blazing fire, seeing forms come and go, thinking over problems, remembering loved ones is an important psychological activity, but one not always possible in today's centrally heated homes. However, television, suitably programmed, could easily take over this hypnotic function, helping to develop, as it were, 'the third eye' within ourselves.

Beyond the Horizon

As a result of the integration of various digital technologies, our reach, previously limited to our immediate environment, is being extended to the ends of the earth. We shall have access to a source of experiences far richer than we have ever known. Our power to know, to communicate and to influence will be greater than any generation that has gone before. It will be up to us to take intelligent advantage of the incredible opportunities such developments present for enriching and enhancing our lives.

103

Artist's Hideaway

"Hallo? You're looking for an illustration to show *what?* Hang on, I'll take a look in my files." Behind a curtain of rushes I find what I need. "No problem. I knew I had just the thing tucked away here somewhere."

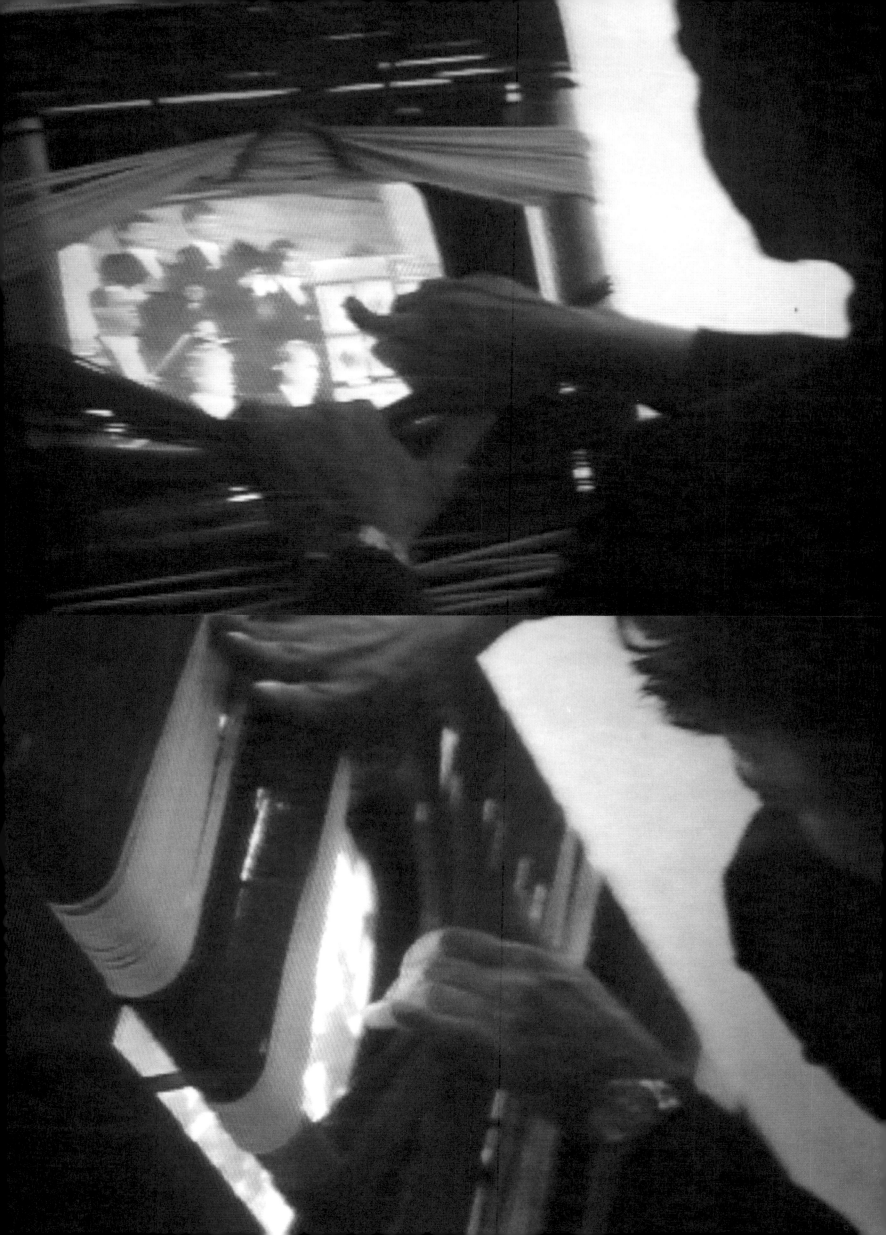

Given its central role in domestic ritual and its embodiment of our shared culture, I was intrigued by the idea of television as a modern totem. This set explores that notion in a very literal manner.

Invisible but ever-present within a vertical, highly coloured sculpture, a helpful and comforting spirit waits patiently to be consulted from time to time. We know it is there, and when we need its advice, we respectfully part the richly textured strands to reveal its face. The rest of the time, the spirit watches over us, peeping out through the strands; but it does not interfere unless asked.

Francis Chu

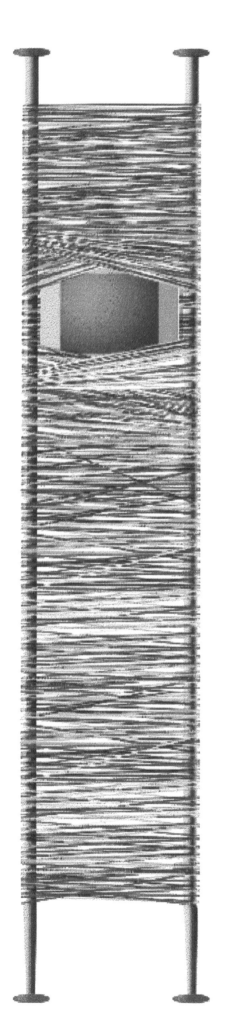

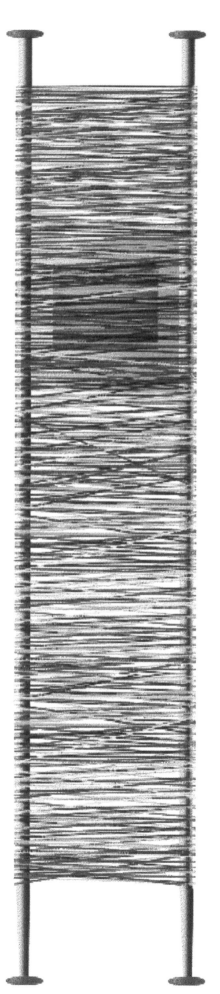

Early bird

As we wake, the birdie-camera shows us today's
weather. We shave, watching the news, then check
the job ads. Looks promising: let's go and see.
Bye bye, tweetie-pie!

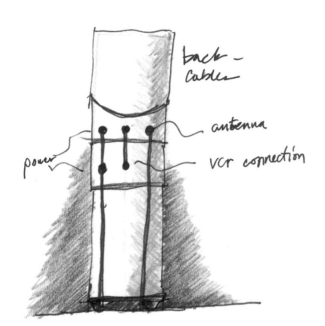

back-cables

power

antenna

vcr connection

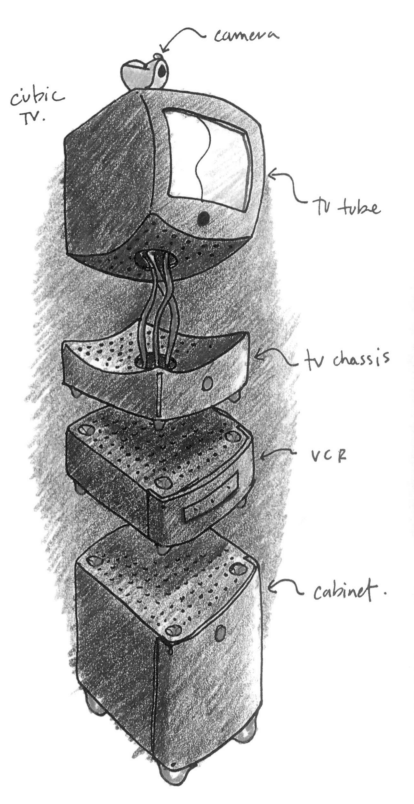

camera

cubic TV.

tv tube

tv chassis

VCR

cabinet.

I envisaged a product developing along natural patterns of growth, rather than a closed path. This set has an unobtrusive, modular design which allows for the addition of options, such as video, telephony, CD-i, Photo-CD, computer and audio, to create truly multi-media functionality. It is a living television. Never turned off, it will merge quietly into the background when we don't want it around and emerge as a companion when we do.

Khodi Feiz

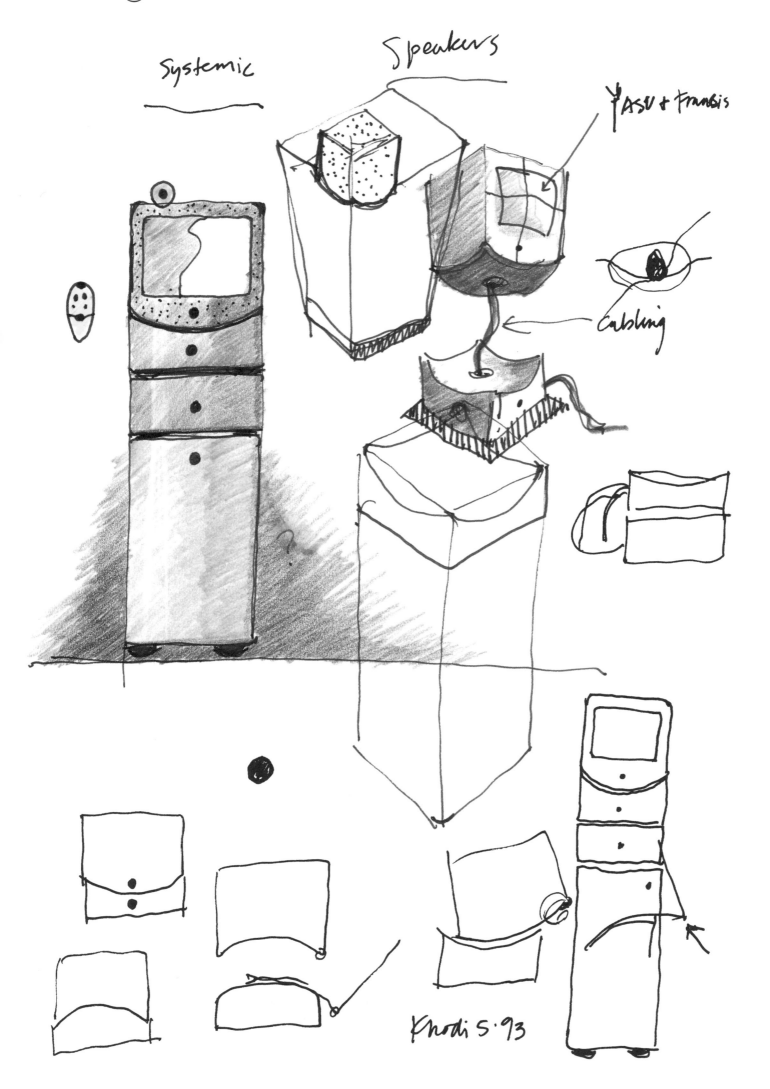

Systemic

Speakers

YASU + Francis

Cabling

Khodi S. '93

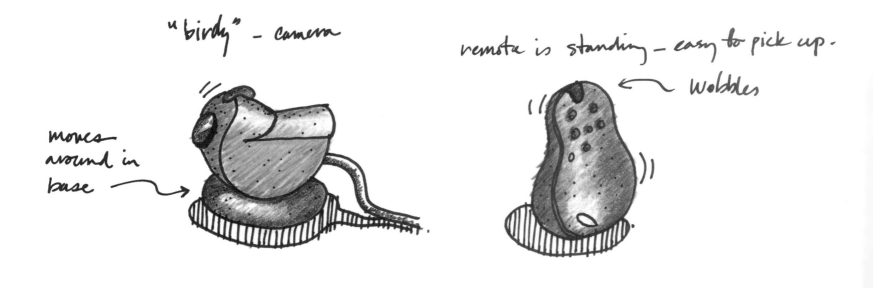

"birdy" – camera

moves around in base

remote is standing – easy to pick up.

wobbles

A modular system can easily spawn
an uncontrollable spaghetti bowl of
wires. By properly managing and
integrating cables, we not only create
a cleaner look but also guide the user
through the confusion of connections.

Khodi Feiz

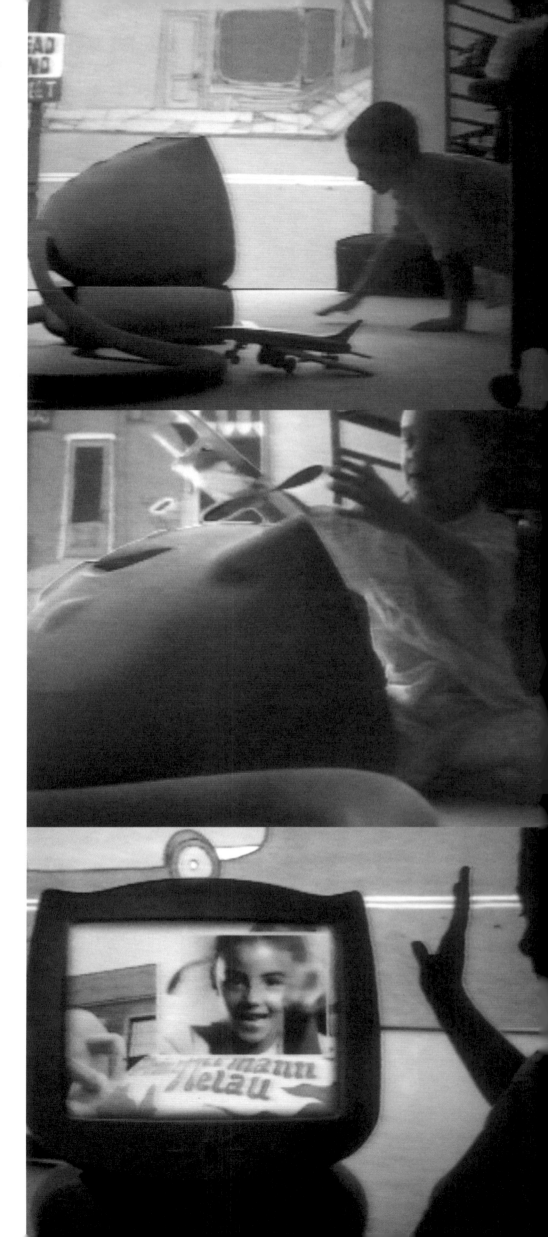

Many consumer products today are lifeless packages of technology, bought, consumed and then thrown away, often with no sense of loss. We need to generate greater affection between the user and the product. I sought to do this by introducing a sense of personality, spirit and warmth into the set by evoking associations with the cat and the mouse, two creatures whose close domestic relationship is familiar all over the world.

Graham Hinde

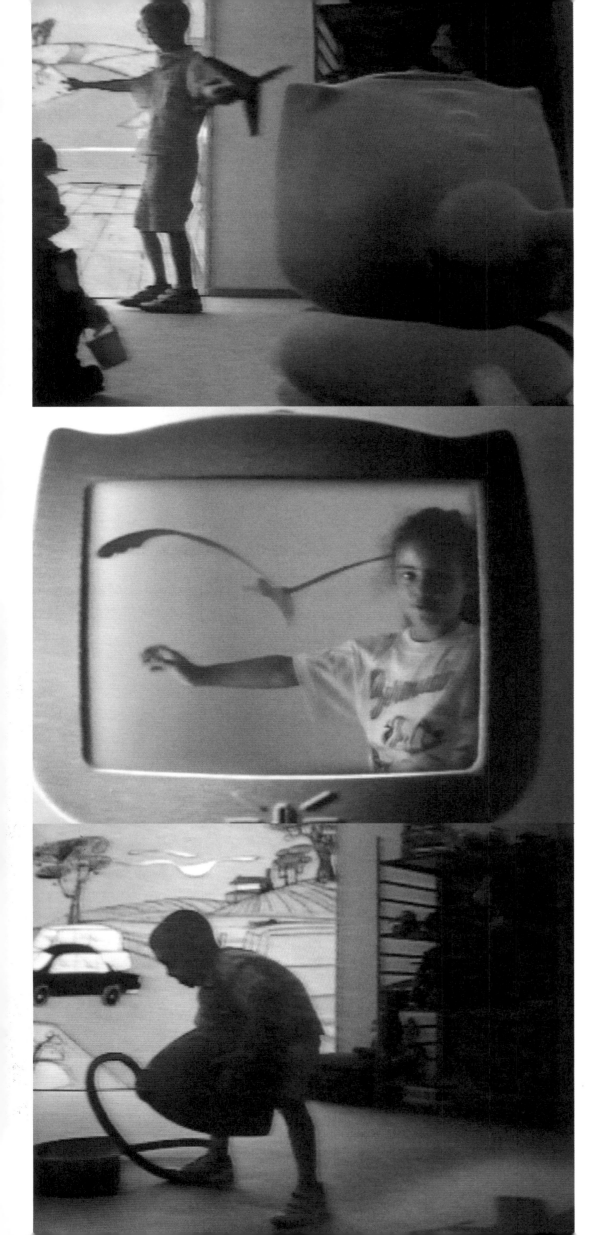

It is a highly portable and flexible combination. The Cat may sit on a table or bed, for example, while the Mouse can hide underneath these objects. The two 'animals' are joined together by their 'tails', which contain the cables they need to communicate with each other.

Graham Hinde

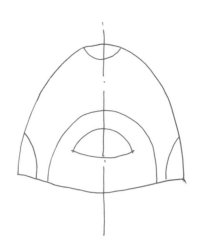

Playing cat and

mouse

"Hey, wanna play today?" says the friend, calling through the Cat and Mouse TV, "I've got a great new plane." "Brilliant! Let me get mine. Neeaaauuuuwwwwwmmmmmm!"

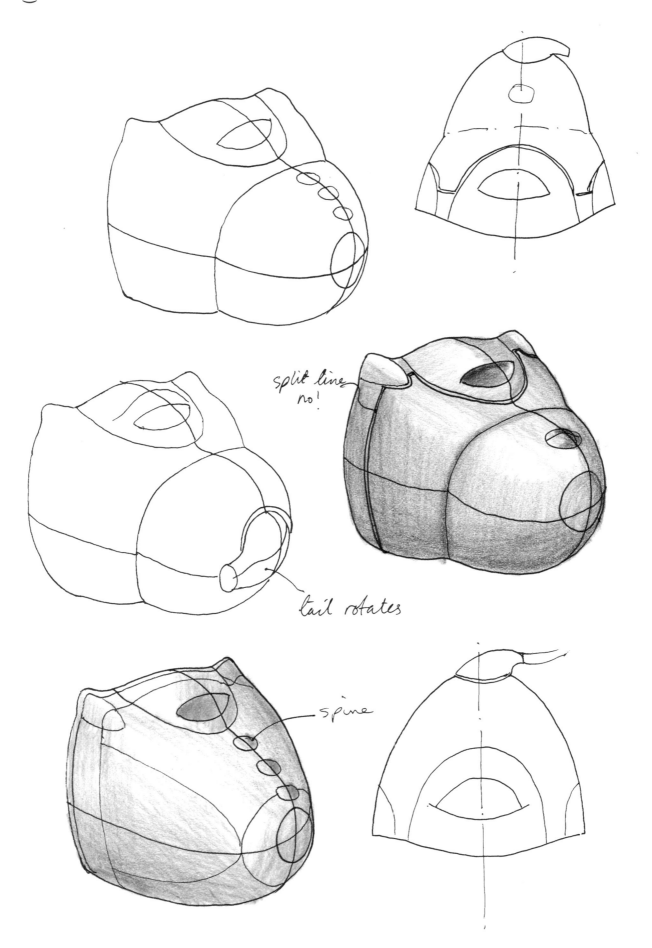

split line
no!

tail rotates

spine

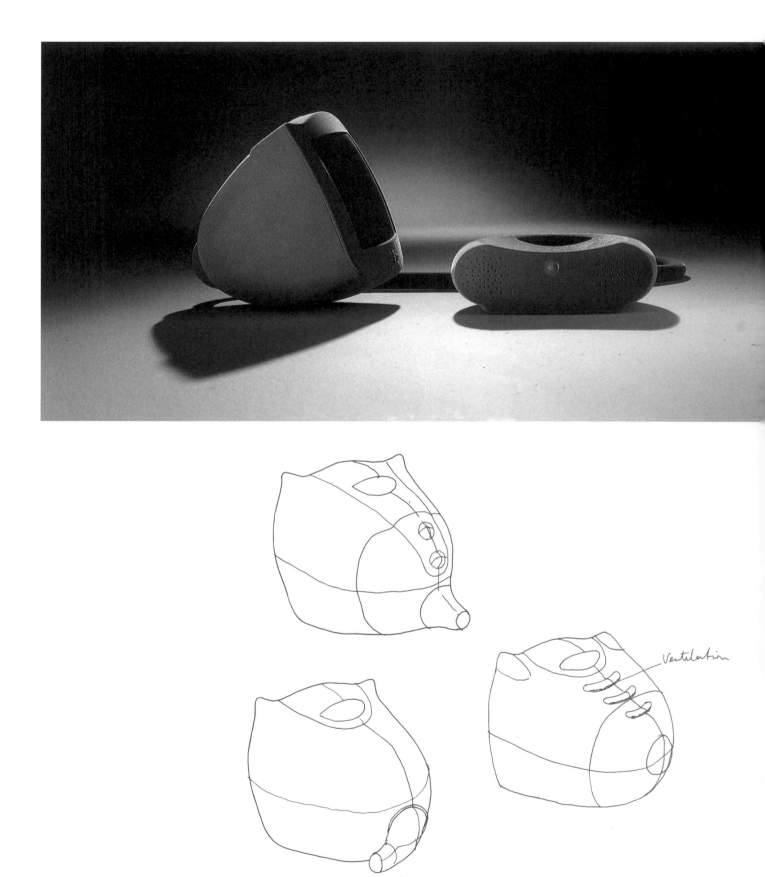

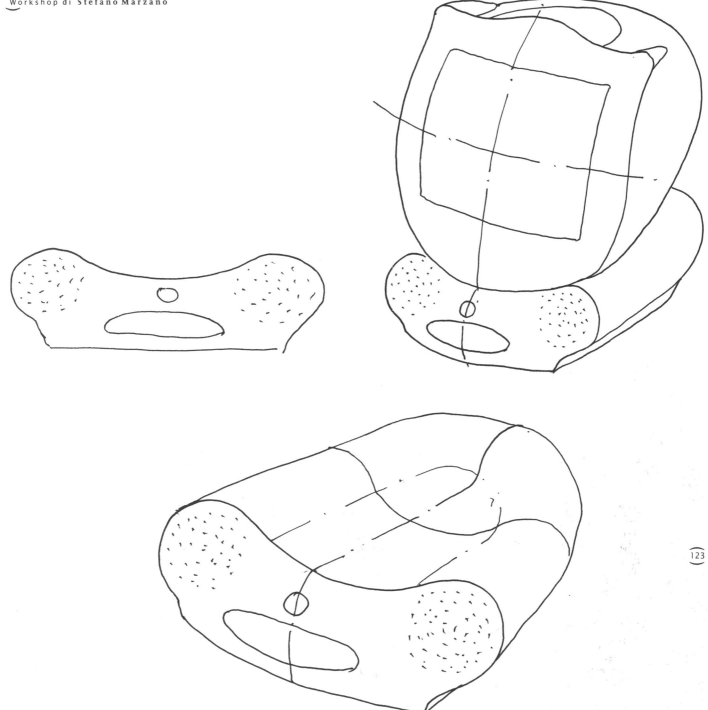

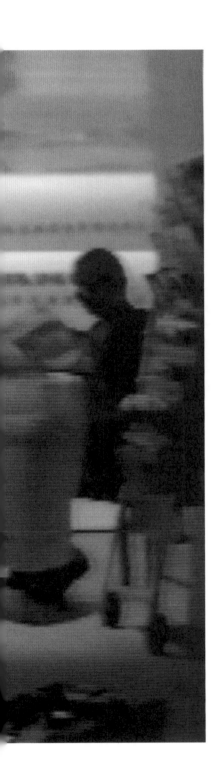

At a video-table in the departure lounge, we have

information and entertainment at our fingertips.

We check our schedule and enjoy a video film about

our destination.

Destination

known

Representing a crystalline amalgam of concepts, this set is capable of systemic, technical transformation over time. It is upgradeable so that it will always be capable of relaying the latest in media programmes. Its longevity will induce confidence in the user and inspire a new sense of loyalty and affection. It can also change on a day-to-day or even minute-by-minute basis, now passive, now active in the user's life. But its true purpose remains intact: to feed the most important of human senses – vision. It is this consistency that will attract more functions.

Lacides Marquez

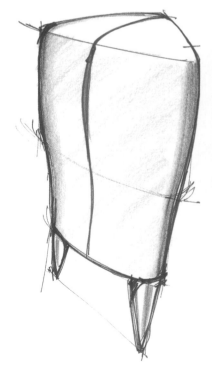

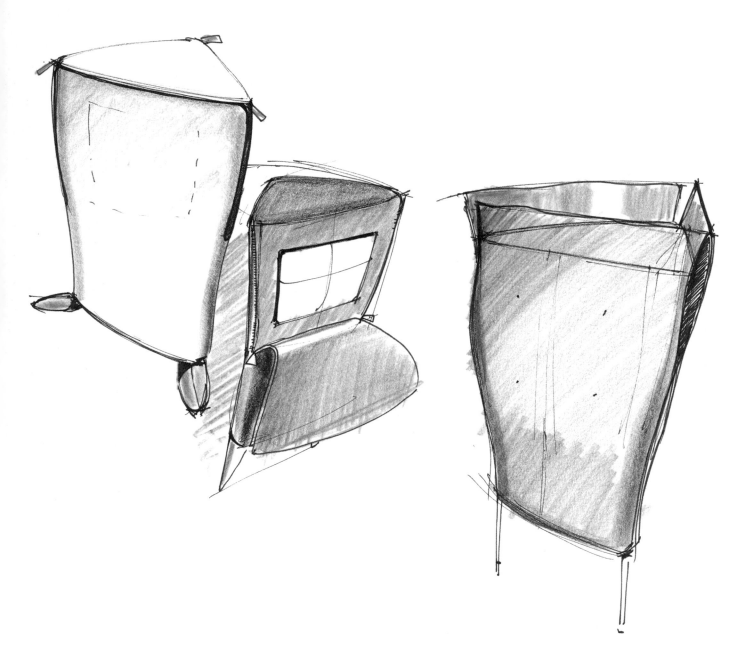

Tactical retreat

When a chess partner withdraws, CD-i jumps into the breach. The knights advance, and play approaches reality.

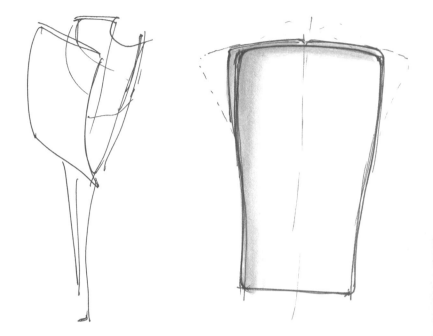

The set's meditative and hypnotic qualities are conveyed through the use of subtle, ambient audio and video images to soothe the user. They are enhanced, too, by its formal purity, reminiscent of the purity of a Japanese garden.

Lacides Marquez

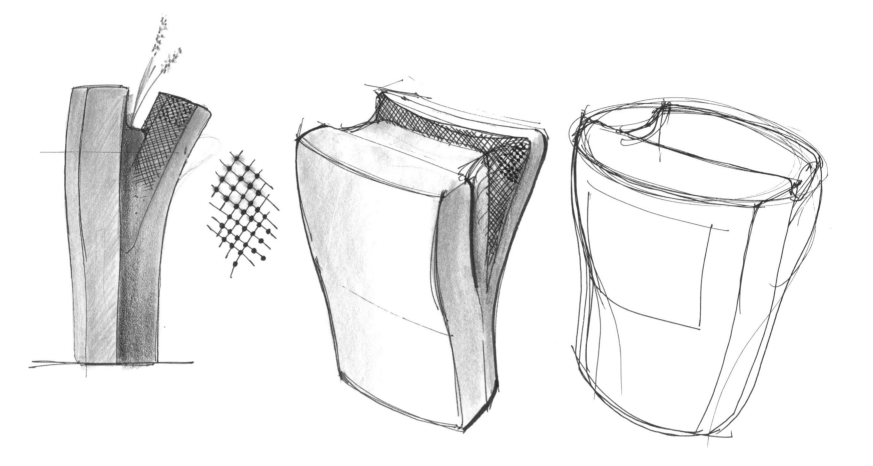

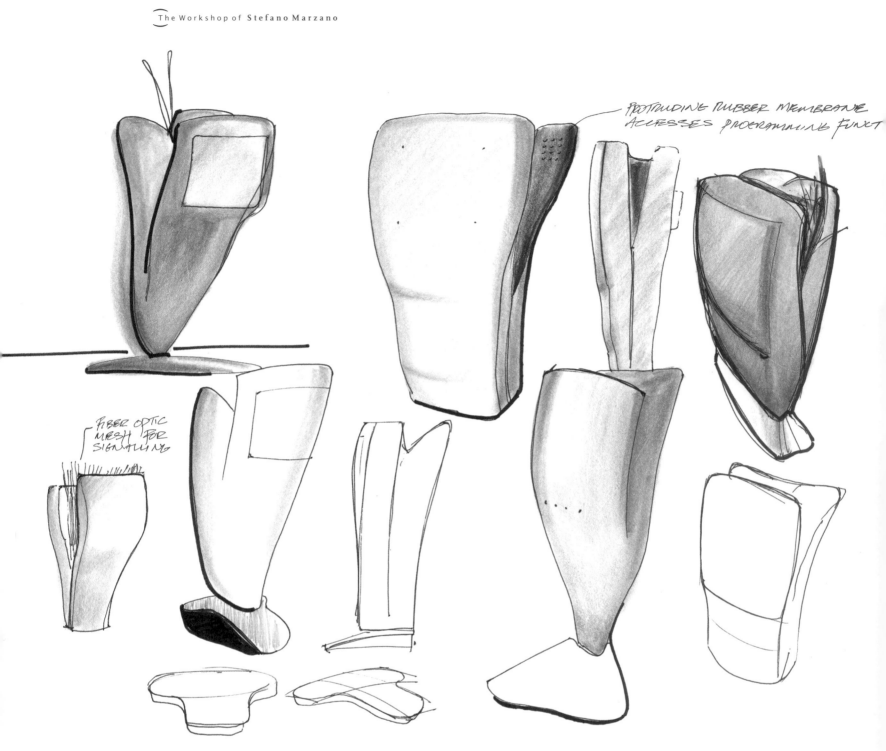

PROTRUDING RUBBER MEMBRANE
ACCESSES PROGRAMMING FUNCT

FIBER OPTIC
MESH FOR
SIGNALLING

PROTRUDING RUBBER MEMBRANE
ACCESSES PROGRAMMING FUNCT

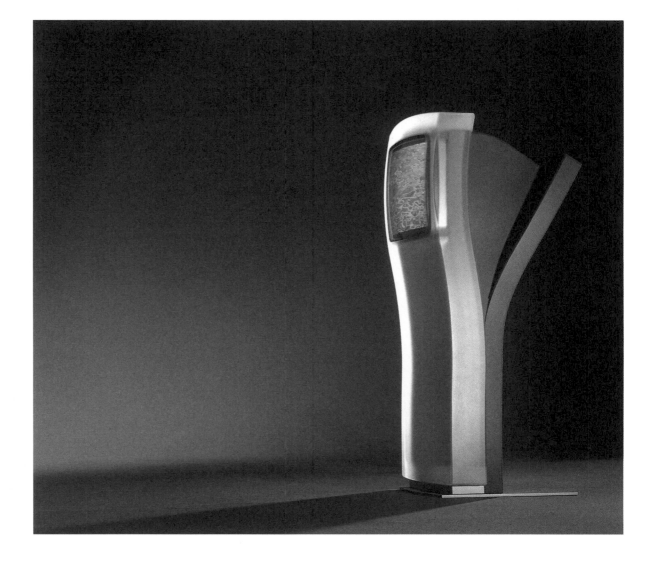

Whether on or off, through its interactive functionality, the set establishes a new relationship between itself as an object, its surroundings and, most importantly, the user.

Lacides Marquez

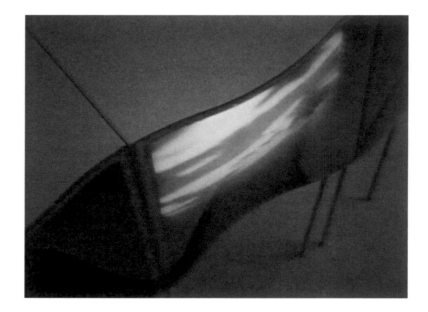

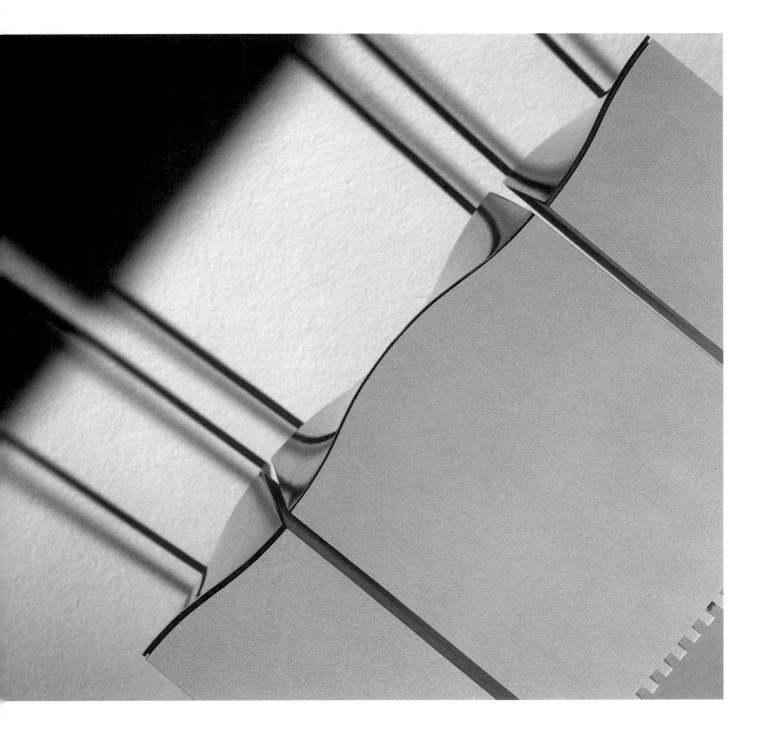

We considered the hypnotic quality
of Zen gardens and how television
might capture that sensation. I was
drawn to the image of the wave
pattern created by a gentle breeze
wafting over a calm pond. In a sense,
I myself was being hypnotised by the
idea of the hypnotic quality of a
product.

Francis Chu

Mindwaves

Time to relax with the Wave TV. Choose your

preferred soothing environment from the menu.

On screen appears a marine ambience – complete

with flying fish.

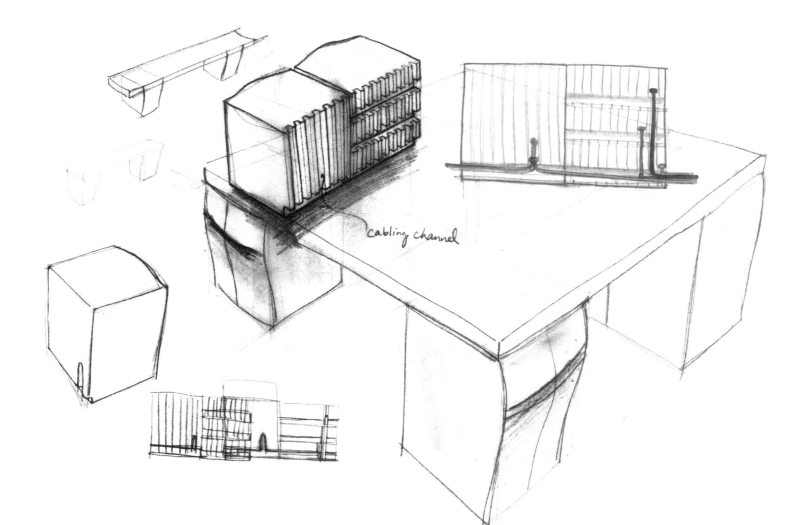

cabling channel

Following a suggestion of Stefano Marzano's, the pattern of overlapping waves on the front is extended to the back, where it serves to guide and conceal the cables. A simple touch, but one that made me realise that the logical interpretation of a functional element may be quite different from its emotional interpretation. Logic we need, but it's emotion we want – even in the most unlikely of places, like the back of a television set.

Francis Chu

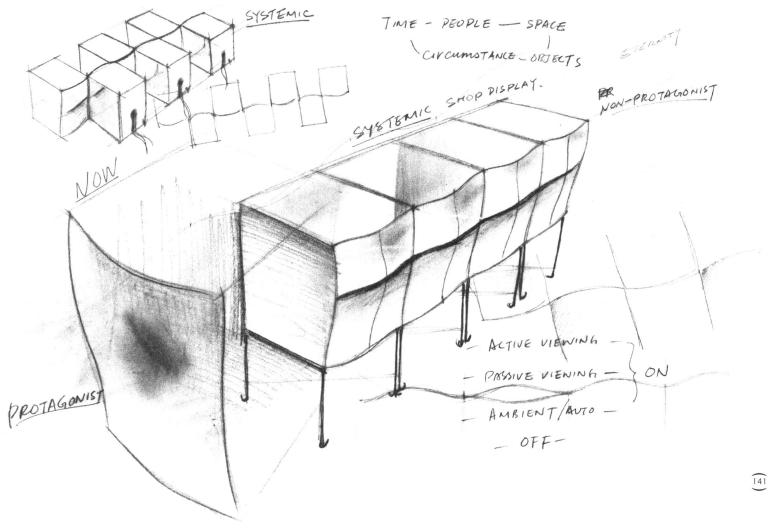

SYSTEMIC

TIME — PEOPLE — SPACE
CIRCUMSTANCE — OBJECTS
ETERNITY

SYSTEMIC. SHOP DISPLAY.

RR NON-PROTAGONIST

NOW

PROTAGONIST

ACTIVE VIEWING
PASSIVE VIEWING } ON
AMBIENT/AUTO
— OFF —

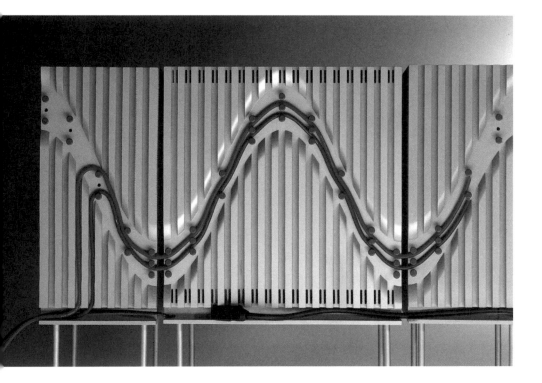

Relaxing by the electronic hearth, we read as TV

lights our page. Great, there's slapstick comedy on

tonight. Hey, watch what you're doing with that

water! ... Now look what you've done: the fire's

gone out!

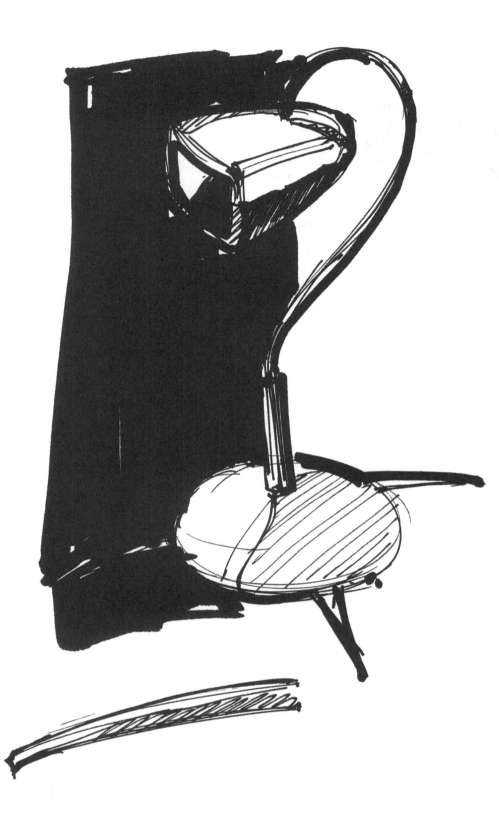

Cosy fire

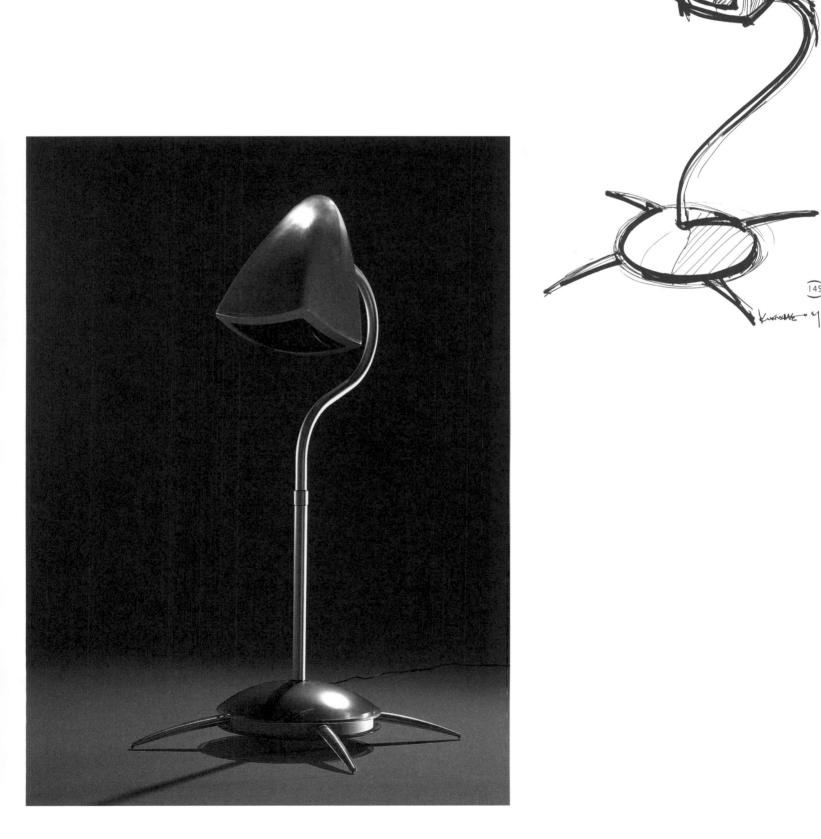

145

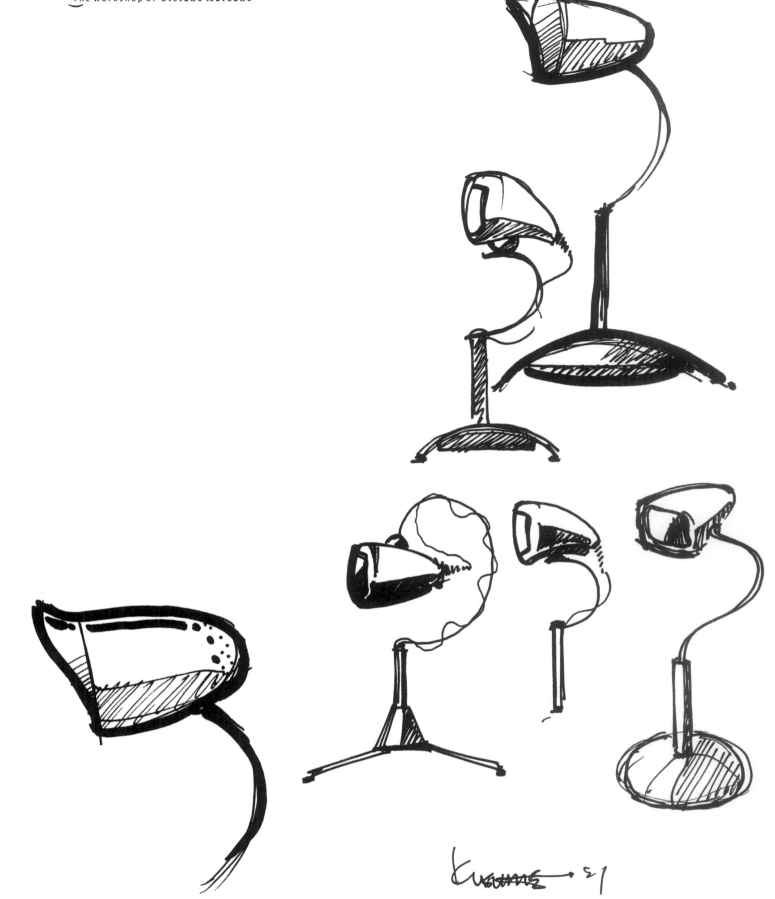

Meet Mis Spring. She'll be your
companion, sharing your home.
Sometimes she'll play a leading role
in your domestic drama, at other
times she'll take a back seat or go to
sleep, leaving you or someone else to
be the star. But she's always ready to
entertain you at a moment's notice.
As she grows older, you can educate
her and give her new clothes. That
way, she'll stay with you longer.

Yasu Kusume

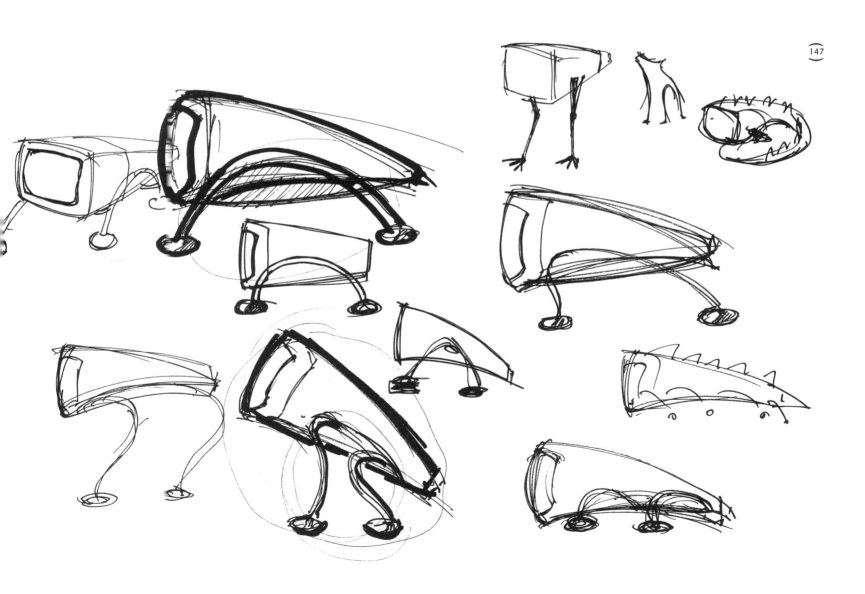

Crisis and Growth:

Industrial Design and

the Creative Tradition

Andrea Branzi

Crisis ard Growth

The changes affecting our planet at this time are also sweeping through the world of Design. Although it may seem only a small and marginal world, it is in fact to be found at the heart of every profound transformation that has marked the history of this extraordinary twentieth century.

The roots of the culture of Design can be traced back to the two contrasting concepts of crisis and growth, concepts so typical of the modern age. Indeed, concern with them characterises the current state of design, too. It is completely absorbed in the process of thoroughly revising the old, nineteen-eighties model of development, while at the same time laying the foundations for a different frame of operation, one that will enable a new model of development for the future to be devised. It is not therefore just the outward signs of international design that are changing, but also – and above all – its methods, its organisations, and the relationships it forms.

Two Models

Moments of crisis have always provided the opportunity to launch a new model of 'growth' by means of a profound restructuring of industry. When the West found itself facing the first great recession in the modern industrial economy towards the end of the nineteen-twenties, the way it surmounted it was to develop new models of growth, in which, for the first time, design was assigned a leading role. Europe emerged from the Great Depression by embarking on a process of forced industrialisation. However, this took place within a society hemmed in by great dictatorships (of both right and left) and in a market where the growth of consumption was controlled. European design of that period developed a vision of a physical world that could be reconstructed by adopting the logic of the factory and not of the market, for human beings who were seen as producers (and not consumers), and in a single-logic society, with a rational and controlled growth in consumption.

The United States of America emerged from the same crisis of the thirties with a completely different model of growth. Through Roosevelt's New Deal, the country strived for a restructuring of social consumption that would lay the foundations for a new and egalitarian 'affluent society'. It was to be a society based on the laws of the free market and favouring the growth of mass consumption. It would have a new morality and the satisfaction of the consumer would at the same time be the fulfilment of both society and state.

Even before the Second World War, then, design in the United States had chosen to take a direction of its own, one based on the search for narrative forms of great allure and in which the mass diffusion of the myth of modernity played a significant part. The partners of American design in this process were not the protected economy, but the free market, not the worker, but the consumer, not dictatorships, but democracy, and not the rational product, but merchandise.

These two different models came into armed conflict in 1944, when US troops landed as part of the Allied forces in Normandy and Sicily. They imported with them the first elements of the consumer society into Europe, along with all the behavioural and philosophical, not to mention stylistic and industrial, innovations that that society entailed. Yet it was to take another twenty years before the culture of consumption was accepted and exploited in our Old World. And this was to take place in a manner that was still highly critical, with reservations of both an ethical and social nature. This restraint

In Europe, design followed a model that regarded people as 'producers'. In North America, however, it was directed at the 'consumer' and aimed at the development of an affluent society.

was in line with the tradition of European design, born as it was as a mediation between industrial and humanistic culture.

Other historical changes were required, such as the second great economic crisis of the early seventies, for the European consumer goods industry to be able to adapt in structural, and not just quantitative, terms to the American and Japanese models. In fact, the end of that crisis saw the emergence not only of the new model of post-industrial growth, but also of a new structure of the market and a new culture of design. The response to the industrial and social crisis of those years consisted in a sweeping programme of technological restructuring, involving the introduction of electronic technology into production cycles and the computerised management of retail stores. The automation of assembly lines made it possible to introduce diversified mass-production runs to meet the demands of an increasingly fragmented and contradictory market, in which traditional income-based divisions gave way to variegated patterns of consumption and divergent life styles to which the old mass-production systems were no longer capable of responding.

New Design

It was within this new operational framework that design carried out its first philosophical revolution, accepting the idea of products that were not universal in appeal but were able to select their own users: products with high figurative content, products in ranges devised for markets with various tendencies, products able to pass freely from high to low technologies, or from definitive products to provisional ones – and vice versa.

All this was given, during the nineteen-eighties, the name of New Design. It was based on two contrasting models of operation. On the one hand, there were the ever larger and increasingly important design centres within the major industries producing consumer goods, such as automobiles, computers and electrical appliances. Their energies were completely taken up with the task of introducing electronics into manufacturing cycles and user interfaces in an increasingly competitive market. These internal design centres were sensitive to the tumultuous changes taking place in markets, but also inclined to reject as subversive the cutting edges of the linguistic and methodological renewal which the new culture of design was freely experimenting with and spreading throughout the world.

New Design led to the creation of independent centres to carry out advanced research into new cultures of habitation. Large design centres within industry focused on the application of new electronic technologies to systems of production.

On the other hand, the New Design of the eighties was also promoting new and autonomous centres of experimentation, such as Alchymia, Memphis, and the Domus Academy. These took on the task of carrying out independent research into new cultures of habitation and new types of merchandise. With a few isolated exceptions, the major industrial organisations remained impermeable to these new possibilities. Culturally biased against such alternatives, the companies were wholly concerned with perfecting and specialising existing types of merchandise, rejecting advanced experimentation with anything that was felt to be too innovative.

The End of an Era

The crisis that we have been experiencing in the early nineteen-nineties has once again dealt a hard blow to design in its role as the champion of an optimistic vision of a mature post-industrial society. In some ways, indeed, it seems as if what is really in crisis is that very model of exclusively qualitative growth of Western industry which design has developed. It is being shaken to its roots by the claims that new areas of poverty are making on the wealthy countries, blocking their search for more and more sophisticated qualities with the threat of social and environmental breakdown. And today's crisis is a truly difficult one because, unlike the crises that preceded it, it not only has an effect on the economic front but also on the industrial model of production and the geopolitical structure of the planet.

The elements that need to be brought together to trigger a new phase of growth are slowly being formulated, and deserve to be followed closely. They have new consequences for design too, and provide some interesting keys to the interpretation of the discipline's current difficulties as part of an evolutionary process.

The crisis in the Communist regimes and their subsequent collapse has set the seal on a historical era that began with the French Revolution of 1789; an era that saw the birth of modern politics, based on social conflict and on the notion that these conflicts can always be resolved in a definitive manner, through a revolution that would set up an alternative system to the existing one.

This historical era, which lasted for 200 years, is now over. We are living in an age of great complexity, one marked by deep conflicts. But the system we live in no longer has alternatives outside itself: it is a mono-logical, planet-wide system, differentiated solely on the basis of territory. It is a system, therefore, in which post-industrial capitalism has won; but it remains characterised by a high degree of fragility, owing to the political and environmental limits which threaten it. We have thus entered a cultural period whose most noticeable feature is the planet-wide scale of its problems, a period founded not on certainties, as in the fifties, but on uncertainties, on unresolved problems, on the unanswered and unanswerable questions that are the same the world over.

With the alternative model of Communism having proved a dismal failure, our system now has to rely for its growth and survival on its capacity for continuous self-examination, on its ability to review and reform without a break, so as to find new strategies of development and balance. And consequently, in this difficult period, the culture of the design project is acquiring a new political dimension, and a new sense. It is no longer concerned with proposing radical alternatives to the model of industrial development, but instead it seeks to revise and reform it, to provide new areas of growth that will make it possible to overcome the social and environmental crises typical of a mature industrial society: a society in which it seems as if everything has been designed, but whose present and future are still waiting to be given shape.

Thus, the century of the Historical Avant-Garde is drawing to a close, and that of the Permanent Avant-Garde is beginning; a century in which avant-garde movements will be required to work within the mechanisms of the system, as a critical driving force, as a creative approach to the problem-solving that can lead to the realisation of new growth.

Positive Polarities

It is within this new context that the model of design operation, based on the bipolarity that existed in the eighties between the major industrial design centres and the independent centres of experimentation, is being reconstituted in a vast programme of collaboration, in which the industries' own centres are opening up to a relationship with the external powerhouses of design, the creative studios. In this collaboration the latter are assigned tasks that are not directly concerned with design. Instead, what they are being

In the 1990s, the crisis affect ng the whole planet is bringing the two poles of the design worlc – industrial design centres and creative studios – back together in a new phase of development.

asked to do is use their capacity to describe broad scenarios and general problems, from which may be derived new types of products and new cultures of use. These new products will enter a market that is at one and the same time flooded with and starved of guiding commodities, i.e., commodities that can both relieve the congestion resulting from the now general overabundance of goods on offer and form new islands of meaning based on more solid and lasting sets of values.

La Bottega dell'Arte

La Bottega dell'Arte is a pioneering example of this new approach to design. In it, Philips asks designers from outside the company to conduct a series of workshops focusing on particular problems, with the aim of generating new hypotheses on the future of a mature product, such as the television set. The company's internal design structures will then work on these ideas to develop new products. It is a way of working that allows Philips to maintain the lines of its own product policy, to make use of its own great technological and typological experience, and to accumulate know-how that would otherwise inevitably be dissipated in temporary external consultancy. At the same time, the outside forces called on to collaborate with the company will not have to develop inappropriate and alien technological skills, but will be able to retain all their own experimental agility, confronting it positively in the workshop with the indispensable capacities of the company.

When we speak of a new model of growth to get us out of the crisis of the nineties, therefore, we are referring to a number of elements in business and design culture which can be brought together in a much larger 'laboratory', one in which the industrial system of the West is engaged in the task of defining its own future. This cannot be a repetition of the past, but must be an improvement on it – a challenge to the present.

The great industrial restructuring on which Europe has already embarked is defined in part by a new set of laws and standards designed to protect the environment. These laws are leading to the development of new processing technologies and different ways of designing objects, based not only on new types of interface but also on their recyclability at the end of their useful life. This is a genuine revolution in the design of industrial products, taking place within the framework of balanced, environmentally-friendly growth in a market conforming to international standards.

The *La Bottega dell'Arte* workshops are part of the process of developing design in order to deal with the crisis and changes that are under way.

But the on-going industrial restructuring is also being defined by new types of merchandise. After the total replacement of mechanical devices by electronic ones, and the functional improvements introduced during the nineteen-eighties, the market now requires new product lines. Just such a search for new products formed the motivation of the workshops described elsewhere in this book. But this search, now under way, is not being undertaken in an effort to increase consumption in an indiscriminate and pointless manner. Rather, the aim is to restructure the market, to develop a new ecology of the natural and artificial environment, and to create islands of meaning that define consumption not as a category of the ephemeral and provisional, but as a solid culture for a democratic and reformed society, one in which a new generation of tools will be able to liberate people from uninspiring work, encouraging mass creativity and individual freedom.

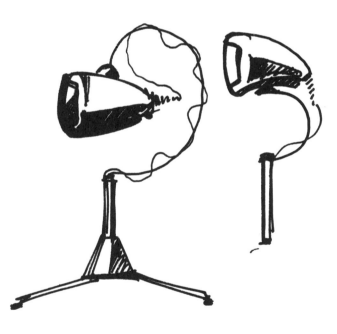

The Contributors

Andrea Branzi

Andrea Branzi, architect, designer and critic, was born in Florence, where he also studied. He now lives and works in Milan. His work ranges from radical architecture in the 1960s, to his current collaboration with some of Italy's most advanced industries. He has worked for many of Italy's prestigious design firms and design-related companies. In 1983 Branzi founded the Domus Academy, the first international Graduate Design Centre, of which he is now Vice President. He is a member of the European Community Commission for the Development and Promotion of Design in Europe, and in 1987 he received the Special Golden Compass Award for his work as designer and theorist. Branzi's furniture design, architecture and urban planning are celebrated throughout the world. He has had one-man exhibitions in Italy, France, Germany, Japan, Brazil, the United States and Canada, and he recently won the international competition for the future lay-out of the site of the Berlin Wall. Andrea Branzi is the author of several books on design and is a regular contributor to periodicals such as *Casabella* and *Modo*.

Derrick de Kerckhove

Derrick de Kerckhove is Director of the McLuhan Program in Culture & Technology and teaches in the Department of French at the University of Toronto. He holds doctorates from Toronto (in French Language and Literature) and Tours (in the Sociology of Art). He was an Associate at the Centre for Culture & Technology and worked with Marshall McLuhan as a translator, assistant and co-author for over a decade. De Kerckhove is the author and editor of a number of books on the interrelation of culture, technology, biology and cognition, including (with Charles Lumsden) *The Alphabet and the Brain* (1988) and *La civilisation vidéo-chrétienne* (1990). His most recent book, *Brainframes: Technology, Mind and Business* (1991) addresses the differences between the effects of television, computers and hypermedia on corporate culture, business practices and markets. Derrick de Kerckhove is currently exploring a new field of artistic endeavour, linking art, engineering, and emerging communication technologies.

Stefano Marzano

Stefano Marzano is Senior Director of Philips Corporate Design. He holds a doctorate in Architecture from the Milan Polytechnic Institute. During the early part of his career, he worked on a wide range of assignments for several designers and design firms, including Makio Hasuike, the Philips-Ire Design Centre, Pavesi & Pavesi, and Design Broletto, of which he was co-founder. In 1978 he joined the Philips Design Centre at Eindhoven, The Netherlands, where a year later he became Design Leader for Data Systems and Telecommunication products. He returned to Italy in 1982 to direct the Philips-Ire Design Centre (Major Domestic Appliances), becoming Vice President of Corporate Industrial Design for Whirlpool International (a joint venture of Whirlpool and Philips) in 1989. In 1991 he took up his present post in The Netherlands. Stefano Marzano is on the staff of the Domus Academy, Milan, and is a member of the Academy's Strategic Committee. He is also on the Advisory Board of Domus Design Agency, a joint venture of the Domus Academy and Mitsubishi Corporation, and a member of the Governing Body of the Eindhoven Academy of Industrial Design.

Alessandro Mendini

Alessandro Mendini was born in Milan in 1931. He is an architect, writer, painter, and one of the most talked-about and respected theorists in the world of design. He has been editor of the periodicals *Casabello*, *Modo*, *Domus* and *Ollo*, and his books include *Paesaggio Casalingo* (Domestic Landscape), *Architettura Addio* (Farewell to Architecture), and *Progetto Infelice* (An Unlucky Project). Examples of his work can be found in several international collections, including those of the Metropolitan Museum and the Museum of Modern Art in New York, and the Centre Pompidou in Paris. Mendini approaches each design project as a work of art and each work of art as a design project, exploring a sensibility that ranges from radical utopianism to straightforward design. From time to time he comes up with such provocative epithets as 'sentimental robot', 'hermaphrodite architecture', 'universal cosmetics', 'computer handicrafts', and 'pictorial design'. Although he has been the target of much sharp criticism, many young designers revere him for breaking away from prevailing styles and inventing creative solutions for living design in the nineteen-eighties.

Francesco Morace

From 1981 to 1986 Francesco Morace, sociologist, was a researcher for GPF & Associati. As part of the 3SC Monitoring program, he specialised in mass communication, fashion and furnishing. In 1988 he founded Trends Lab, a research institute specialised in applying sociocultural changes and market trends in marketing research and strategic planning. He teaches socio-economic forecasting at the Domus Academy, Milan, where he is Head of the Department of Fashion. He regularly conducts courses and seminars at L'Institut Français de la Mode (Paris), CFP (Carpi), DAMS Art Academy (Bologna), the Universidad Internacional Menendz Pelayo (Madrid) and the Politecnico (Milan). He is also the author of a number of essays, including *Chi ha lasciata il segno?* (1988) and *Controtendenze* (1990). He is also co-author of *I boom: Società e prodotti dell'Italia degli anni '80* (1990) and *Iperspesa: La distribuzione e i consumatori nel supermercato del 2000* (1990). Francesco Morace is a regular contributor to periodicals such as *Modo*, *Gap Casa*, *Interni*, *Design Diffusion*, and *Forme*.

Paul Bas

Paul Bas was born in Belgium in 1960. He graduated in Product Development from the Nationaal Hoger Instituut voor Bouwkunst en Stedebouw, Antwerp, in 1983. He joined Philips Corporate Design in 1989 and now works at the Philips Corporate Design section in Bruges, Belgium. He has attended numerous workshops in Europe and North America.

Roland Bird

Roland Bird was born in Britain in 1967. He received the degree of BA in Design for Industry from Newcastle upon Tyne Polytechnic in 1991. During his studies, he fulfilled work placements in Britain at STC Telecommunications and the London firm, Addison Design Consultancy. He joined Philips Corporate Design in 1991 and is currently working on television design.

Wa Francis Chu

Wa Francis Chu was born in China in 1960. He is a graduate of Hong Kong Polytechnic and holds the degree of Master in Industrial Design from the Royal College of Art (London). Following periods of work for design firms in Britain and the United States and for manufacturers in Hong Kong and Britain, he joined Philips Corporate Design in 1989. His work has been shown at international exhibitions and featured in British and US publications.

Khodi Feiz

Khodi Feiz was born in Iran in 1963. In 1986, he graduated from Syracuse University (USA) in Industrial Design. For the next four years he worked for the Texas Instruments Design Center. In 1990 he joined Philips Corporate Design where he is currently a senior product designer. He also lectures at the Eindhoven Academy of Industrial Design. His work has received a number of awards.

Graham Hinde

Graham Hinde was born in Britain in 1960. He graduated from Kingston Polytechnic in 1983 in Furniture and Related Product Design. He joined Philips Corporate Design in 1984 where he has worked on audio and video products, personal information products, interactive media and communications systems.

Yasushi Kusume

Yasushi Kusume was born in Japan in 1961. He is a graduate of the Musashino College of Art (Tokyo) and the College of Design, Pasadena, California. After working as a freelance graphic and product designer for various design firms in Los Angeles, he joined Philips Corporate Design in 1989. He is currently specialising in television design.

Benny Leong

Benny Leong was born in 1961 in Macau. He is a graduate of the Swire School of Design (Hong Kong) and the Royal College of Art (London). After working for various companies in Japan and Hong Kong, he joined Philips Corporate Design in 1991. His work has won several prizes and has been featured in publications in Britain, the USA and the Far East. He is currently working on the design of domestic appliances.

Lacides Marquez

Lacides Marquez was born in the United States in 1957. He is an industrial design graduate of the Pratt Institute, having earlier studied Mechanical Engineering and Design at the University of Wisconsin. He has worked for several firms in the United States, where he specialised in furniture, exhibition design and telecommunications products. He joined Philips Corporate Design in 1987. He is currently working on television design.

Bertrand Richez

Bertrand Richez was born in 1962 in France. Following studies in Textiles, Art History and Architecture, he graduated from the École Superieure des Arts Décoratifs (Paris) in 1987. He subsequently worked as a designer for French companies manufacturing sunglasses and domestic appliances. He joined Philips Corporate Design in 1992, where he is currently concerned with the design of lighting.

Jane Worthington

Jane Worthington was born in Britain in 1969. She is a graduate of Carlisle College of Art and Design and Leicester Polytechnic. In 1991 she joined Philips Corporate Design, where she currently works in the Commissions Group.

Design and layout
Cees de Jong, Jan Johan ter Poorten
V+K Design, The Netherlands

Printing
B.V. Kunstdrukkerij Mercurius-Wormerveer,
The Netherlands

Editorial support
Andrew Baxter Associates, The Netherlands
Nicoletta Branzi, Italy

Photography
Orsola Branzi, Italy
Jos Jansen, The Netherlands
Korff & Van Mierlo, The Netherlands
Rik van den Wildenberg, The Netherlands

Modelmaker
KEMO B.V., The Netherlands

Videos
Studio Azzurro, Italy

Acknowledgements
Practical assistance provided by the following
companies in The Netherlands is gratefully
acknowledged:
Silicon Graphics Computer Systems; Parametric
Technology Corporation; Electro GIG Nederland B.V.;
Maestrocad B.V.